D0789485

THE BEAUDOIN EASY METHOD OF IDENTIFYING WILDFLOWERS

Over 475 Mountain Flowers

By
Viola Kneeland Beaūdoin

Color Photos by Genevieve Berry
Illustrations by Elizabeth Houser

Front Cover Photo—Yellow Stemless Evening-Primrose

Library of Congress Catalog Card Number 83-72033

ISBN 0-9611960-0-9

Second Printing

Evergreen Publishing Company
Aurora, Colorado

Printed by Quality Press
Englewood, Colorado

In Loving Memory
of my Mother
Emma Kneeland
who loved beauty in all things

With deep appreciation of the encouragement given me by my wonderful family: Richard, Florence, Wayne, Deanna, Linda, and Tom. Without their support and assistance, there would have been no book.

Special thanks to Genevieve Berry for her excellent photography, often obtained under difficult conditions but always done carefully and cheerfully.

CONTENTS

YELLOW FLOWERS

OTHER FLOWERS

HOW TO IDENTIFY A FLOWER

Step 1. Select the color.

Step 2. Select the shape.

Step 3. Select the Quick Reference Box that—except for size—exactly describes your flower and plant.

Step 1. COLOR

Red includes pale pink thru rose and scarlet to dark wine.

White includes pure, waxy white to off-white or somewhat dirty white.

Blue includes pale blue and lavender through deep purple.

Yellow includes deep cream to dark orange.

Other includes all colors not described above, such as gray, green, brown, flesh.

Step 2. SHAPE

To determine shape—ALWAYS check in the following order:

1. DAISY Does your flower resemble a button with a row of fringe around it? (Either thick or scanty fringe).

The flower center resembles a button because it is so densely packed with what look like coarse threads of even or uneven length. The fringe around the outside is formed by either narrow or wide, petal-like "rays."

There may be from 3 to 175 rays but the button center is always compact and there are never any separate, slender, freely-moving stamens between the button and the rays.

Sometimes the center has an even row of "threads" raised slightly all around on its edge like a narrow rim on a button, but

1

these are not freely-moving stamens.

Remember—this group (also called Composites) includes many flowers besides daisies; such as sunflowers and asters.

2. SHRUB. If not a "Daisy" type flower, is the plant a shrub with several very woody, branched stems, like a rosebush or a lilac?

3. STALK If plant is not a shrub, are the flowers arranged along the sides of a stalk?

Flowers bloom along the side or sides of a main stem. They may or may not have individual stems, and the stalk may be erect or leaning. The flowers may be of almost any one shape and some may still be in bud while others are blooming.

4. HEAD If not a Stalk, are the flowers arranged at the top of the stem in a Head?

Several flowers, each with its tiny stem (usually tiny) are grouped together at the tip of a stem in a rather wide "cap."

All thistles have been placed in this group. (Prickly Poppy—although prickly—is not a thistle. It has 4 to 6 large petals and many stamens.)

NOTE. In rare cases, the same kind of plant may have flowers blooming along a stalk one year or in one locality but at another time or place may have all its flowers at the top of the stem like a Head.

5. SAUCER If none of the above, but your flower is shaped like a cup, bowl or plate, it is probably a "Saucer."

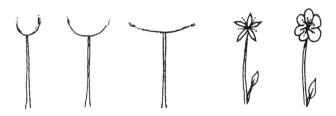

A saucer flower, when it first blooms, often resembles a cup but as it matures, may open out to deep bowl shape, finally becoming a shallow saucer. Flowers vary in this, some open immediately into flat plates; in others, the petals fall while they are still cup-shaped. All 3 shapes are included under the heading, "Saucer." A saucer flower may have three to many petals and several to many slender stamens. It may occur singly on a plant, or in a very loose cluster, or so densely as to cover the plant.

A few saucer flowers have cone-like centers but unlike the Daisy Group flowers, these cones are surrounded by some separated, slender, freely-moving stamens inside the circle of petals.

The dandelion type is included here because it is usually flat like a plate (may sometimes have a slight bulge in the center).

6. MISC. A few flowers, such as Shooting Stars, do not fit into any of these groups. Check for these exceptions in MISCELLANEOUS.

Step 3. QUICK REFERENCE BOXES

Select the box that—aside from size—exactly describes your flower and plant. The flowers are not listed alphabetically, but in each color/shape division are arranged from large to small. It is impossible to give the exact size of any flower. Size is affected by soil, rainfall, altitude, time of year, and other factors. The figures listed are an indication <u>only</u>.

Botanical terms are defined in Key Terms.

EXAMPLE

Riding in the foothills, you notice a large bright yellow flower like the one on the book cover, on a low plant growing on a sloping bank along the roadside. Obviously, it will be listed in the Yellow section of the book, but in which Shape? Glance over the 6 Shape descriptions. Always start with the first shape—Daisy. No, your flower is not a Daisy type. The second shape is Shrub. Your plant is not a shrub. Third shape is Stalk with flowers along the sides of a main stem. Your plant doesn't have any main stem—only a long flower stem. Next is Head, with a number of flowers at the tip of a main stem. This is out. Next is Saucer—shaped like a cup, bowl or plate. Your flower is shaped like a bowl so you turn to the Yellow/Saucer section of the book, and check the Quick Reference boxes.

The first box states:
"2-4″ (or 6″) star flowers, usually white, sometimes pale yellow. Usually 10 petals. Many stamens. A few rough, alternate, "clingy" leaves . . ."

This doesn't fit. Star flowers have pointed petals. Your flower has rounded petals—and only 4 instead of 10. Your plant leaves are neither rough nor alternate. They are all basal (rising from ground level).

The second box says:
"2-4″ waxy, cuplike flowers. Large, shiny leaves float on surface of lakes."

Size is right but your flower is not waxy; its long, rather narrow plant leaves are non-shiny; and the plant is on dry soil—nowhere near water.

The next box says:
"4 large, rounded petals. Bright yellow flower 2-4″ wide. Long yellow stamens. Basal leaves only; lance-shaped. Plant 3-5″ high."

This fits your flower and plant in every detail (because the lance-shaped leaves may or may not have tooth-like projections along the sides) so you have identified a Yellow Stemless Evening-Primrose. (P. 177)

4

There is no need to look further. All the succeeding flowers will differ from yours in some respect, such as cactus plant with no leaves; or 5 or 10 pointed petals; or a spreading vine with opposite leaves. There is a Common Evening-Primrose, related to yours and with similar flowers but differing in having a main stem 6-36″ tall, with alternate leaves.

Also, in each Color/Shape section, the flowers are arranged in decreasing size with small ones at the end.

VARIATION

Flowering dates are as variable as size but most flowers bloom from 3 to 12 weeks sometime during the period of May thru August with the heaviest season in June and July. Dates have been given for those that commonly bloom before May or after August.

Shades of color and locations also vary. The words, "usually", "often", and "about" constantly recur in the descriptions because flowers simply do not conform rigidly to an exact pattern. Also, any species of colored flower may infrequently produce a white blossom.

If the flowers may occasionally be found throughout the Rocky Mountain region, no location is listed for them. Many of these grow in the Black Hills, too.

If your flower does not display all the characteristics (except size) set forth in any one Reference Box then check another shape division—if you are sure of your color.

You are now ready to identify flowers. A paper clip placed on the Key Terms page will be helpful until the Terms are familiar.

SHORT-CUTS

After you have become acquainted with this method, you will find several short-cuts. One that is helpful with all flowers except the Daisy Group is the number of petals. There are usually 3, 4, 5, or 6. The number of petals is listed in many of the boxes, so if your flower has 4 petals you can quickly eliminate every box that says 3, or 5, or 6 petals.

Another short-cut—useful with all plants—is the leaves. If the leaves on your plant are opposite each other (in pairs), you can eliminate every box that says, "Leaves alternate", or "Leaves basal only."

Familiarity with the method will show you other short-cuts.

This book includes over 475 of the most common Rocky Mountain wildflowers.

POISONOUS PLANTS

Although there are occasional references to poisonous plants, no attempt has been made to list all of those that are poisonous—nor all which are edible. The only safe rule is : Don't put anything in your mouth.

Also, unless you know mushrooms well, don't taste them.

KEY TERMS

Alternate—occuring singly; not opposite each other; said of leaves and buds.

Axillary—rising from the axil of a leaf—that is, from the upper angle where a leaf joins the stem.

Basal—at the base; as leaves at the base of a plant.

Bract—a modified leaf—usually small—close below a flower or a flower cluster. Often looks like a sepal.

Calyx—the circle of sepals in a flower.

Clasping—said of a leaf or its petiole if its base partly or wholly surrounds a stem. (Fig.1)

Clawed—said of petals that have very narrow bases.

Corolla—the circle of petals in a flower.

Daisy-Aster distinction. Daisies are often hard to distinguish from Asters. The surest distinction lies in the bracts (on back of flower head).

Daisy bracts are of equal length and they are in 1 or 2 rows. Aster bracts are of varying lengths, are in 3 or more rows, and they overlap unevenly. Townsendia bracts also overlap unevenly. (Fig. 2)

Decumbent—reclining on the ground but with the tip rising. (Fig.3)

Disk flowers—the slender, tubular, tightly packed florets which form thistle heads and also form the center of daisy type flowers.

Entire—having an even margin; as a leaf with no cuts, lobes or teeth. (Fig. 4)

Keel—the 2 lower parts of a pea flower, which are fused together.

Leaflet—one of the divisions of a compound leaf. See Leaf Illustrations.

Linear—long, narrow and flat with parallel margins. (Fig. 5)

Lobe—a division or part of a leaf cut halfway or less to its midrib. Petals and sepals, too, are sometimes called lobes.

Nerve—a leaf vein.

Nodding—said of flowers or buds that hang down. (Fig. 6)

Opposite—in pairs; rising at the same level but separately.

Orchid flower—has 3 petals and 3 sepals but is irregular in shape. The lowest petal is the largest. (Fig. 7)

Ovate—shaped like the outline of a hen's egg; with the broad end at the base.

Palmate—said of a leaf whose leaflets spread out like fingers from the tip of the petiole. (Fig. 8)

Pea flower—has 5 petals; the top petal or "banner" is erect; 2 on the sides are called "wings," and the 2 lower ones are joined in a boat-like keel enclosing the pistil and stamens. (Fig. 9)

Two groups of pea flowers are often confused; the Loco—*Oxytropis* and the Milkvetch-*Astragalus*.

7

Loco flowers have a sharp beak on the keel. Milkvetch flowers have no beak on the keel. (Fig. 10)

Pedicel—stem of an individual flower.

Petal—one of the inner circle of floral leaves or parts of a typical flower; usually white or brightly colored. Petals surround the stamens and pistil.

Petiole—stem of an individual leaf.

Pinnate—said of a leaf with leaflets along both sides of its petiole. (Fig. 11)

Pistil—seed-bearing organ of a flower; composed of ovary, style and stigma. See Flower Illustrations.

Rays—the petal-like florets around the outer edge of such blossoms as asters and sunflowers. Rays may also mean the small individual stems in umbels.

Scalloped—having a series of curves, as the edge of some leaves.

Sepal—one of the outer circle of floral leaves or parts of a typical flower; just below or outside of the petals. Are usually small and green; sometimes large and bright. Sepals protect the flower while in bud. Anemones, clematis and a few other flowers have only bright sepals—no petals.

Sessile—having no individual stem; as a leaf attached directly to a branch or a plant stem.

Spur—a hollow, tubular or sac-like extension of a petal or sepal; as in violets or columbines. (Fig. 12)

Square—having 4 sides; not round.

Stamen—the pollen-bearing organ of a flower, consisting of filament and anther. Stamens sometimes extend out of a flower like hairs.

Tendril—a thread-like, twining outgrowth on stems or leaves; used for climbing.

Terminal—growing at the end of a branch or stem.

Toothed—having small, sharp-pointed projections along the sides, as a toothed leaf. (Fig. 13)

Tube—a hollow, cylindrical structure; especially the tubular, lower part of some blossoms. (Fig. 14)

Tundra—a treeless plain of arctic or subarctic regions.

Two-lipped flower—has 5 petals, 2 of which are joined in an upper lip and 3 in a lower lip. Some species have a large tube. And in several species like Lousewort, the upper lip is hooded and may extend into a beak. (Fig. 15)

Umbel—a flower cluster with all the pedicels rising from the same point—like the spokes of an open umbrella. (Fig. 16)

Whorl—3 or more leaves arranged in a circle around a stem.

Zones—land divisions by altitude. Many flowers grow only at certain altitudes. For the terms, "Foothills-Montane", etc. see Plant Zones. For more details, see Flower and Leaf Illustrations.

Daisy

Fig. 1

Aster

Fig. 2

Fig. 3

Fig. 4

Fig. 5

Fig. 6

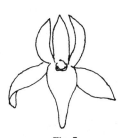
Fig. 7

Fig. 8

Fig. 9

9

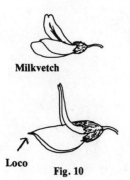

Milkvetch

Loco

Fig. 10

Fig. 11

Fig. 12

Fig. 13

Fig. 14

Fig. 15a

Fig. 15b

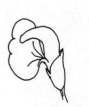

Fig. 15c

Fig. 16

Red Clover
(p. 33)

Bristle Thistle
(p. 30)

Pink Plumes
(p. 47)

Fairy-slipper
(p. 47)

11

Fairy Trumpet or Gilia
(p. 19)

Parry Primrose
(p. 31)

Horsemint
(p. 31)

Wild Geranium
(p. 40)

Lambert Loco
(p. 23)

Fireweed
(p. 20)

Rocky Mtn. Beeplant
(p. 32)

Pink-head Daisy
(p. 15)

Wood-lily
(p. 39)

Queens-crown
(p. 33)

Shooting-star
(p. 47)

IMPORTANT! Check Daisy-Aster distinction in Key Terms.

PINK-HEAD DAISY or Beautiful Daisy *(p. 16)* *(color plate p. 13)*	1-2″ flower. Pinkish wool below the narrow pink rays. Yellow center. Leaves entire, pointed. Plant 8-24″.

Each stem may have 1 to 3 pink-lavender to rose-colored heads. In dry weather they may be very pale. Wrapped around the spreading, re-curving bracts is a densely woolly layer of pink to reddish hairs. The buds, also, are woolly and usually bend down. The blossoms curve up like a saucer—are rarely flat. Leaves are alternate and the upper ones clasp the stem. This is one of the tallest daisies. Its stem is woody and it is common in subalpine meadows. *Erigeron elatior,* Composite Family.

SHOWY TOWNSENDIA *(p.16)*	Rose-purple, grooved rays. Greenish-yellow center. Leaves alternate, gray, grasslike. Erect stems 2-8″.

Rays are notched at tip and the pointed bracts are in about 3 rows. Plant is common on dry slopes, Wyo. to New Mex. Montane-Subalpine. *Townsendia grandiflora,* Composite Family.

SUBALPINE DAISY (See Blue/Daisy Shape)	Rose-purple rays 1/8″ wide. Bracts narrowed at tip and curved outward. Erect stem. Lower leaves petioled. Large yellow center.
EASTER DAISY (See White/Daisy Shape)	Pink, grooved rays. Greenish-yellow center. Leaves gray, grasslike. No plant stem—flowers and leaves rise from roots at ground level.
SUN-LOVING ASTER (See Blue/Daisy Shape)	Rose-purple rays. Yellow center. Loose, leafy bracts. Leaves green. Stems decumbent, 2-8″ long.
CUT-LEAF DAISY (See White/Daisy Shape)	3/8″ flower, pink rays, yellow center. Leaves cut, with 3-forked ends. Low plant. Dry places.

15

Pink-head Daisy

Showy Townsendia

16

WILD ROSE
(p. 18)

5 petals. Fragrant saucer flowers. Leaves alternate; <u>5 to 11 toothed leaflets</u>. Prickly shrub.

Flowers are very pale pink to deep rose color. Have many stamens. In fall, the leaves turn lovely shades of red and maroon. The prickly branched stems are 5″ to 8′ high. The 3 most common species in this area may hybridize. Plains-Timberline. *Rosa arkansana, acicularis,* and *woodsii,* Rose Family.

NOTES. The bright red fruits are called "rose hips." Indians and early settlers ate them. Bears eat them and they are an important winter food for birds.

Rose hips have a high vitamin C content, rating above oranges. Rose water, made from rose petals may be obtained from druggists and can be used in ice cream, syrups and other foods. It has been used in medicine for centuries and is useful in cosmetics. An oil distilled from some species is used in perfume.

Sappho, Greek poetess around 600 B.C. wrote of the beauty of the rose, and roses were cultivated in Greece as early as the 5th century B.C.—were, perhaps, the first flower to be brought under cultivation.

In the days of the Roman Empire, rose water was used in food, wine, and mixed drinks, and the very wealthy sometimes filled their fountains with it.

GOOSEBERRY
(See White/Shrub)

5 separated <u>petals shorter than the sepals</u>. Tube- or bell-shaped flowers. Small, lobed leaves. Prickly shrub. Moist places.

SQUAW CURRANT
or Wax Currant
(p. 18)

5 tiny petals flare out from 1/4″ pinkish tube. Small, alternate, lobed leaves. <u>Rigid stems</u>. Sunny places.

Pink or whitish tube flowers in clusters of 2 to 4. The small red berries are sticky. Leaves, 1″ wide or less, are rounded, often in clusters; and have a characteristic odor when crushed. The shrub, 1-5′ high, is much branched. Common on dry slopes, Foothills-Montane. *Ribes cereum,* Gooseberry Family.

MOUNTAIN-
   SNOWBERRY
(p. 18)

4 or 5 pink petals. Tube- or funnel-shaped flowers. Leaves <u>opposite, thin, rounded</u>. <u>Old bark shreds</u>. Berries are white.

Leaves, 1″ wide, are paler below. The shrub is much branched and

1 to 4' tall. Old bark is shreddy; new growth is light green. Foothills-Montane. From Colo. north. *Symphoricarpos oreophilus,* Honeysuckle Family.

MOUNTAIN-SPRAY
(See White/Shrub)

| Profuse sprays of tiny flowers, white or pink; later turning rust-color. Small wedge-shaped leaves. On canyon sides. |

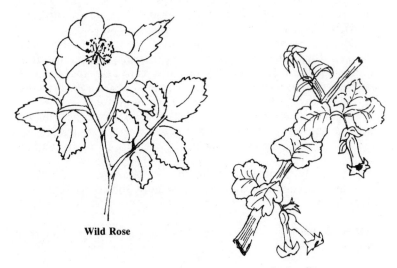

Wild Rose

Squaw Currant

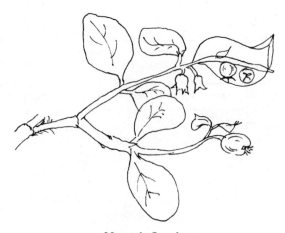

Mountain-Snowberry

18

SHOWY MILKWEED	5 petals. Large, opposite leaves. 3″
or Pink Milkweed	round clusters of 3/4″ pink to whitish
(p. 26)	star flowers. 5 pinkish sepals turn
	down.

Flowers have pointed petals and bloom in showy, crowded clusters ranging in color from deep pink to whitish—rarely greenish-purple. All species of milkweeds have an extra set of floral lobes. First there are 5 drooping sepals; next, 5 petals; then a unique set of 5 petal-like parts called hoods, curving inwards; and last, a unit in the center of the flower formed by the 5 stamens and the pistil which are closely connected. This elaborate arrangement ensures that any visiting insect will catch its feet in the sticky milkweed pollen and carry it to another flower.

The leaves are heavy, lance-shaped to oblong, and 4-10″ long. The veins are parallel with each other but at an angle to the midrib. Many of these big leaves do not fall in autumn but remain on the stem where they dry out and rattle in the wind. Plant is 1-5′ tall, is very hairy, and has milky juice. Usually found along roads and ditch banks, often in clumps. This is the showiest and most abundant of about a dozen species of milkweed in this area. Plains-Montane. *Asclepias speciosa,* Milkweed Family.

NOTES. The plant contains a thick, milky sap or latex. Like flax and dogbane, milkweeds have sturdy fibers that can be made into tough string or cord.

The rough seed pods, 3-4″ long, turn a rich brown and finally split open to release flat seeds tufted with long, silky hairs. Goldfinches use these hairs for nest-building.

Milkweeds have been used in medicine for centuries and the botanical name, *Asclepias,* comes from Asklepios, the Greek god of medicine. Most parts of the Showy Milkweed are edible if properly prepared.

Butterflies are attracted to Milkweed and the green and black caterpillars of the Monarch Butterfly feed on this plant.

PAINTBRUSH	Large cluster of 1-2″ vertically
(See Red/Head)	overlapping, bright reddish "petals."
	Pointed, green tips sometimes protrude above these "petals."

SCARLET GILIA	5 petals. 1-2″ trumpet tube flowers
or Fairy Trumpet	end in stars. Often on one side of
or Skyrocket	stem. Pink sepals. Leaves alternate
or Polecat Plant	and deeply cut.
(p. 26) *(color plate p. 12)*	

Flowers are bright scarlet but one large subspecies varies from

RED/STALK

19

white to pink or coral, and is more common in the lower altitudes. The slender trumpet flares out into 5 narrow, pointed lobes. The numerous flowers are attached mainly along one side of the stem which may lean slightly as though pulled over by the weight of the little trumpets. Leaves have linear, threadlike divisions that are separated and often curved. When crushed, the upper leaves smell like a skunk, hence the name, "Polecat Plant." The stout but slender stem is 1-3′ tall. This plant is biennial, growing a rosette of leaves the first season and a flowering stalk the second year. Gilia grows on dry, sunny slopes, often in large, bright, colorful colonies. Foothills-Montane. Hummingbirds like the flower nectar and with their long bills are well equipped to obtain it. *Ipomopsis aggregata*, Phlox Family.

SCARLET BUGLER or Firecracker Plant or Torrey Penstemon *(p. 27)*	Scarlet tube flowers end in 2 lips (see Key Terms); but do not spread widely. Lower lip turns backward. Leaves opposite, entire. Stem 1 to 3 feet. Dry gravelly slopes.

The 3 lobes of the lower lip curve down. Leaves are often dark; may be tinged with red. Plant has one to several non-hairy stems and grows on canyon sides from southern Colorado to New Mexico and Arizona. Jun-Oct; Montane. *Penstemon barbatus*, Figwort Family.

DARK PENSTEMON (See Blue/Stalk)	1″ tube flowers, end in 2 lips. Very dark wine color; often on one side of stem. Opposite leaves; upper ones clasp stem; basal ones have petioles.

BOUNCING BET (See Red/Saucer)	5 separated petals and a 1″ tube. Clusters of 1″ pinkish flowers. Leaves opposite, entire. Sturdy 1-3′ stems.

FIREWEED or Giant Willow-herb *(p. 27)* *(color plate p. 13)*	4 wide, separated petals, rose to pink-purple saucer flowers. 4 sepals. Long stamens. Leaves alternate, entire.

Little reddish-pink sepals peek out between the bright petals. The style is longer than the stamens. Flowers are attached to the tall stalks by rather long pedicels and the lower flowers bloom first so one stem may have at the same time long seed pods, blossoming flowers, and at the top, a number of buds. Leaves are narrow, willow-like, veiny (see Alpine Fireweed following) and from 2-5″ long. They have a prominent midrib, and they turn red in autumn.

The one or several unbranched stems are 1-6' tall and they turn reddish as they age. The pods look like <u>large red darning needles</u> and when they open, the seeds float away on little, silky, white parachutes. Jun-Aug. Foothills-Timberline. *Epilobium angustifolium,* Evening-Primrose Family.

NOTES. Fireweed is a valuable forage plant, eaten by deer, elk, and livestock. It was a favorite with grizzly bears when they still roamed over this region.

This is one of the most attractive and widespread plants of the mountain area. It is called Fireweed because it tends to rush into burned-over districts and also onto disturbed land like roadsides, thus converting devastated sections into places of beauty. It was used for this purpose in the bombed-out districts of London.

ALPINE FIREWEED—is similar to the preceding but is a shorter plant with larger flowers and <u>short,</u> broad, grayish leaves, <u>not veiny.</u> Also the style is <u>shorter than the stamens.</u> It grows in moist soil near timberline. Is often leaning rather than erect. *Epilobium latifolium,* Evening-Primrose Family.

MOUNTAIN HOLLYHOCK	5 petals; 2″ saucer flowers. <u>All leaves alternate</u> with 5 to 7 <u>deep lobes,</u> toothed. Plant 2-7′, in clumps.

Flowers rose-purple or pinkish-white. Leaves heart-shaped or rounded. Montane-Subalpine; chiefly on West Slope. *Illiamna rivularis,* Mallow Family.

WILD HOLLYHOCK—is similar but its flowers are 1″, <u>upper leaves</u> are round and scalloped or shallowly lobed; <u>lower leaves are</u> deeply, palmately divided. Plant is 8-36″. Foothills-Montane. *Sidalcea neo-mexicana,* Mallow Family.

LANCE-LEAVED FOUR-O'CLOCK	Many rose-purple saucer flowers* open in late afternoon. Leaves opposite, broad, entire, pointed. <u>Hairy,</u> bushy plant 1-3′.

*Actually several small flowers with no petals are enclosed in a brightly colored shallow cup of petal-like bracts. Plains-Montane; dry ground. One species has linear leaves. *Oxybaphus hirsutus,* Four-O'Clock Family.

BROOMRAPE (See Red/Misc.)	Pinkish, 2-lipped tube flower. Leaves like scales. <u>No green on plant.</u> 6″ or less.

21

LEWIS MONKEY-FLOWER or Red Monkey-Flower *(p. 27)*	2-lipped, rose-red flower, 1-1/2″ wide. Leaves opposite, thin, sessile, slightly toothed. Near water.

Flower is sometimes pink or blotched. Has 4 stamens, and 2 yellow-haired ridges in flower throat. Ovate to oblong leaves. Unbranched, 1-2′ stems. It grows, often in clumps, along mountain streams and in other moist places in northern Colo., Wyo. and Mont. Montane-Subalpine. It was named for the leader of the Lewis and Clark Expedition. *Mimulus lewisii,* Figwort Family.

JAMES SAXIFRAGE or Purple Saxifrage *(p. 27)*	5 "clawed" petals* rose-purple flowers. Leaves alternate, rounded, scalloped. In rock crevices. 6″ or less.

*Clusters of brilliant flowers with "clawed" petals—i.e., each petal has a broad blade but is very narrow at the lower end, thus leaving a wide space between the petal bases. Leaves 1″ broad. Grows in granite crevices or on granite shelves, usually out of reach. It is found only in the mountains of central and north central Colo. Montane-Subalpine. *Telesonix or Saxifraga jamesii,* Saxifrage Family.

COPPER MALLOW or Scarlet Globemallow or Cowboy's Delight *(p. 27)*	5 petals. Clusters of 1 to 1-1/2″ salmon-colored saucer flowers. Leaves alternate, gray, divided. Plant 4-10″. Dry ground.

Flowers are salmon or orange-red and look like tiny hollyhocks. The petal bases are greenish. Leaves are deeply divided and plant is silvery-gray. Plains-Montane. *Sphaeralcea coccinea,* Mallow Family.

NOTES. The marshmallow originally used in cooking was made from the gummy juice of one species of mallow.

The family also includes hollyhocks, hibiscus, okra, and cotton.

PURPLE LOUSEWORT (See Blue/Stalk)	Rose-purple, 2-lipped flower (see Key Terms). Upper lip compressed on sides and strongly arched. Leaves narrow and doubly scalloped. In wet places.

LAMBERT LOCO
or Colorado Loco
(p. 27)
(color plate p. 13)

Pea flowers 3/4″ long, with sharp beak (see Key Terms). Rose to purplish. Leaves basal only; many silvery leaflets, usually in pairs.

Flowers tilt upwards and they all open at about the same time. This is one of the most beautiful and conspicuous flowers in the region, often found in large, bright colonies. It blooms most profusely in July but may occasionally be seen as late as October. Since Lambert Loco and the white Rocky Mountain Loco hybridize, one may sometimes find patches of loco in shades of rose, pink, or lavender.

The leaves, composed of narrow, oblong to rounded leaflets, are shorter than the flower stalks and are gray-green to silvery with flat silky hairs. Plant usually has several flower stems 6-14″ tall. Pods are either erect or spreading—they do not hang down. Plains-Montane. *Oxytropis lambertii,* Pea Family.

NOTES. This and some other locos are poisonous to livestock, although the animals do not eat locos if other browse is sufficient. Occasionally a horse becomes an addict, turns "loco" or crazy, loses weight, and dies.

The pea family is one of the largest plant families and it ranks next to the grass family in economic importance because many of its members, such as peas, beans, clover, and alfalfa, furnish a vast amount of food for man, and forage for animals.

SHOWY LOCO
(See Blue/Stalk)

1/2″ pea flowers with sharp beak. Lower buds open first. Leaves basal with leaflets in rows (whorled). Silvery-silky foliage.

LITTLE-RED-ELEPHANT
or Elephantella
(p. 27)

1/2″ flowers have upcurved beaks resembling an elephant's trunk. Leaves narrow and deeply cut, like a comb. In wet places.

The spike is densely covered with pinkish-purple flowers whose long, upcurving beaks resemble an elephant's trunk. One can even imagine the little elephant's bald forehead and flapping ears. The leaves have purple-tinted margins. Several unbranched stems 6-24″ tall, are clustered together in marshy meadows. Jun-Aug, Montane-Alpine. Is most common in the Subalpine zone. *Pedicularis groenlandica,* Figwort Family.

| **GAURA** (p. 27) | 4 "clawed" petals. <u>Loose clusters</u> of pink and white spidery flowers; showy stamens. <u>Leaves alternate</u>. Plant 1 foot or less. |

The upper ends of the 4 sepals turn back down and flare out loosely. These reflexed sepal tips, together with the protruding stamens and the clawed petals which are very narrow at the base, give the flower a spidery appearance. The petals turn red with age. Leaves are narrow, somewhat toothed, and pointed. Plant usually has several stems and is found in dry places, often along roads. Montane-Alpine. May-Jul *Gaura coccinea,* Evening-Primrose Family.

| **LOVE GENTIAN** or Amarella or Rose Gentian (p. 28) | 4 or 5 petals spread out like a star from a small tube with <u>fringe in its throat</u>. Leaves opposite, sessile. Plant 2-16". |

Flowers are rose-lavender or rarely white. Leaves are pointed and entire. The stem may have several erect branches. This frail, variable plant is found in moist places; Montane-Alpine. At high altitudes it may be only 1 or 2" tall, with just one little blossom. *Gentiana* or *Gentianella amarella,* Gentian Family.

| **SPREADING DOGBANE** (p. 28) | 5 petals. Small pink bell-flowers with red veining inside. Leaves opposite, entire, shiny, and <u>drooping</u>. |

These dainty little bells sometimes hang in pairs. In fall, the leaves turn golden. The branching stem is straw-colored to reddish-brown; has milky sap and is 8-24" tall. In sunny, rocky locations, Foothills-Subalpine. The long, very slender seed pods are in pairs. *Apocynum androsaemifolium* and *A. medium,* Dogbane Family. (The leaves of Apocynum medium usually <u>spread out</u> rather than droop.)

INDIAN HEMP—*Apocynum cannabinum* is similar to Dogbane but is taller, has smaller, white to greenish flowers (no pink), and its leaves spread or turn up but <u>do not droop</u>. These 3 species hybridize freely, and they have tough fibers similar to those of flax. Indians made string and rope from Indian Hemp.

| **HOUNDSTONGUE** | 5 petals. Spiral clusters of 1/4", dull red flowers, hiding among the alternate, entire, <u>soft-hairy</u> leaves. Stout, branched plant 1-3'. |

Flowers dull red to reddish-purple. Leaves oblong to lance-shaped. Plant covered with soft, white hairs. Fruits are burs. Plains-Montane *Cynoglossum officinale,* Borage Family.

WIRY MILKVETCH or Limber Vetch *(p. 28)*	1/3″ pink pea flowers (see Key Terms) in long clusters. Top petal arched. Narrow leaflets. <u>Spreading stems.</u> Dry soil.

Flowers are small and pink—or yellowish. The calyx is hairy with a few black hairs and the banner is strongly arched backward. Leaves have 11 to 25 linear to oblong leaflets. Stems are somewhat wiry and 6-20″ long. Plant is common on dry ground, often among sagebrush. Foothills-Montane. *Astragalus flexuosus,* Pea Family.

GAYFEATHER or Blazing Star *(p. 28)*	Small heads of feathery, rose-purple flowers along stem. Each pistil has 2 twisted, thread-like appendages. Leaves alternate, linear, rough-edged.

Flowers appear feathery or frizzled because of the 2 appendages at the tip of each pistil. Gayfeather has disk flowers only—there are no rays or petals. Both flowers and leaves are very thick. The unbranched, rather woody stems are 6-24″ tall. Common from July to Oct. Plains-Montane, in open fields and dry places along the eastern slope of the Continental Divide. *Liatris punctata,* Composite Family.

PINK-FLOWERED PYROLA or Swamp Wintergreen *(p. 28)*	5-petaled, 1/4″ <u>flowers hang along top half of stem. Green, curved pistil protrudes.</u> Pink and white buds. <u>Leaves basal only, rounded, shiny.</u>

Several to many pink flowers. The pistil curves out and then up. Leaves are thick-textured, dark green and 1-2″ in diameter. Plant, 5-12″ tall, grows in damp forests and along streams, Montane-Subalpine. Chiefly on the eastern side of the Continental Divide. *Pyrola asarifolia,* Heath Family.

WILD MINT or Field Mint *(p. 28)*	Clusters of tiny, pale, 2-lipped flowers <u>in leaf axils.</u> Protruding stamens. Opposite leaves. Square stems. Mint fragrance. In moist soil.

The flowers, lavender to pale pink, are in dense axillary clusters.

RED/STALK

Although 2-lipped, they are slightly irregular. Leaves are lance-shaped, toothed, and pointed, with prominent veins on back. Plant is 4-15″ tall. Plains-Montane. Its fragrant leaves are used to flavor beverages. This mint is a circumpolar species. *Mentha arvensis,* Mint Family.

NOTE. If the flower clusters are at the ends of the square stems, compare with Spearmint in White/Stalk.

ALPINE SORREL *(p. 28)*	Tiny red or greenish flowers look like flat seeds; are very thick. No petals or rays. Leaves kidney-shaped (or round). Plant 2-16″.

The seed-like flowers hang along the stem in very dense clusters. They may be red or green or both. The fruits are thin and flat with tiny wings and, like the flowers, may be red or green. Leaves, rising from base of plant, are fleshy. The smooth, erect stem grows in cold, wet places around rocks near and above timberline, Jul-Sep. Plant also grows in Alaska, Greenland and Eurasia. *Oxyria digyna,* Buckwheat Family.

GROUNDSMOKE or Babysbreath *(p. 28)*	4 petals; tiny pink flowers. Very narrow, alternate leaves. Delicate plant 3-12″ tall and intricately branched.

The tiny petals are pink or white, and the leaves are 1/2″ long. Plant has very slender, delicate, closely intertwining branches. It grows on sandy slopes and in dry fields. Foothills-Montane. *Gayophytum diffusum,* and others, Evening-Primrose Family.

Showy Milkweed

Scarlet Gilia

Scarlet Bugler

Fireweed

Lewis Monkey-flower

James Saxifrage

Copper Mallow

Lambert Loco

Little-Red-Elephant

Gaura

Love Gentian

Spreading Dogbane

Wiry Milkvetch

Gayfeather

Pink-flowered Pyrola

Wild Mint

Alpine Sorrel

Groundsmoke

PAINTBRUSH	Cluster 2-5″ long of 1-2″ vertically
or Indian Paintbrush	overlapping, bright red "petals."
or Painted Cup	Small, pointed, green tips sometimes
(p. 37)	protrude above these "petals." 5
	species follow.

Five common species of red paintbrush found in this area all share the following characteristics:

They look like a flower with big, wide, overlapping petals; but the brightly colored "petals" are actually leaflike bracts in various shades of red; and these partially or completely hide the true flowers, which are small, green, and tubular with 2 tiny lips, one of which curves down over the other. Although the leaves have no teeth they are often lobed. The different species cannot be identified by color alone because there is so much variance. May-Sep. Plains-Alpine.

1. **WYOMING PAINTBRUSH**—The bracts are bright red. Protruding conspicuously 1/2″ or more above them are the tubular, pointed green flowers, which are often touched with red. Leaves are linear or cut into linear lobes. The stems are branched and are 1-3′ tall. Plant often grows near sagebrush, usually on dry ground and chiefly in the montane zone. Found Wyo. to Ore. and south to New Mex. and Calif. *Castilleja linariaefolia*, Figwort Family.

   NOTES. This is the Wyoming state flower.
      Paintbrush is somewhat parasitic and often obtains part of its food from the roots of other plants.

2. **ORANGE PAINTBRUSH** or **FOOTHILLS PAINT-BRUSH**—Bracts may be orange to bright red, are broader than the leaves, and are mostly entire. The tubular, green flowers may peek out or may be completely hidden. Leaves are narrow, hairy, usually entire, and often folded. The stem is 4-14″ tall and covered with matted hair. Plant is most common on dry ground in the foothills. Found Wyo. to Ore. and south to New Mex. *Castilleja integra.*

3. **NELSON PAINTBRUSH**—The bracts are divided into narrow lobes and are usually red; may be tipped with yellow. The green flowers may or may not show. The upper leaves, at least, are divided into narrow lobes. Plant is hairy and may be erect or decumbent. Plains-Montane, usually in dry soil, Wyo. to New Mex. *Castilleja chromosa.*

4. **SCARLET PAINTBRUSH**—The bracts are scarlet, and at least some of them are deeply lobed. Some may be entire with an acute tip. Leaves are lance-shaped and mostly entire. The stems

are usually unbranched. This species prefers damp soil and is most common in the montane zone. Throughout the U.S. Rockies. *Castilleja miniata.*

5. **ROSY PAINTBRUSH**—The bracts may be rosy, crimson, pink, purplish, or even two-toned. They are <u>usually entire with a blunt tip</u>, but are <u>sometimes shallowly-lobed</u> with a <u>wide middle lobe.</u> Leaves are narrow-ovate, and mostly entire. Plant is usually unbranched. Although this is a subalpine species, it often grows above timberline, generally in damp soil. Because of plant variation, distinction between Rosy Paintbrush and Scarlet Paintbrush may sometimes be difficult. Throughout our Rockies. *Castilleja rhexifolia.*

SHOWY MILKWEED (See Red/Stalk)	5 petals. 3″ round clusters of 1″ pink to whitish <u>star flowers.</u> 5 pinkish sepals <u>turn down.</u> Large, opposite leaves.

BRISTLE THISTLE or Nodding Thistle or Musk Thistle *(p. 37)* *(color plate p. 11)*	1-1/2 to 3″ flower puff, pink to purple. <u>Projecting, wide, sharp-pointed bracts.</u> Spiny-edged leaves <u>green on both sides.</u> Spiny plant.

Flowers are rose-pink to light purple, and fluffy in appearance. They are distinguished by the sharp, projecting, hairless bracts. The blossoms, on long stalks may be either erect or nodding. Because this is a thistle, the head consists of disk flowers only; long, fluffy ones. The leaves are alternate, rather narrow, 3-6″ long, and deeply lobed. Plant is 2-5′ tall, is very spiny and is winged by down-curved leaf bases. It grows abundantly along roadsides and in waste areas. Plains-Foothills. It is attractive to butterflies and other insects. *Carduus leiophyllus,* or *nutans,* Composite Family.

BULL THISTLE (See Blue/Head)	2″ rose-purple flower puff. Bracts are spiny and <u>cobwebby.</u> <u>Spiny tissue down stem below each leaf.</u> Leaves stiff-hairy above; woolly-hairy below. Spiny plant.

WAVY-LEAF THISTLE *(p. 37)*	1-1/2 to 2″ rose-purple flower puff on long stem. <u>Bracts are green, spiny and tightly over-lapped.</u> Leaves paler below, <u>their bases clasp stem.</u> Spiny plant.

Flowers are fluffy puffs, rose-purple—or sometimes whitish. No hair on the bracts. The flowers, usually solitary, are at top of stem and the ends of branches. Like all thistles, the heads consist of disk flowers only; very long ones split into narrow divisions. Sometimes a pale, dingy-white puff is found among the colored flowers. Leaves are large, deeply cut, and toothed, the teeth being tipped with spines. Plant is 1 to 3-1/2 feet tall, gray-green, hairy and spiny. This is one of our most abundant thistles. Plains-Montane. *Cirsium undulatum,* Composite Family.

NOTE. The botanical name, Cirsium, means "swollen veins," from the use of thistles in ancient times for treatment of swollen veins.

CANADA THISTLE (See Blue/Head)	Numerous rose-purple flower puffs at stem ends, 3/4″ wide—only half as big as the 3 foregoing thistles. Firm, green, spiny bracts form a base 1″ long. Leaves green both sides. Spiny plant.
HORSEMINT or Monarda or Bergamot *(p. 37)* *(color plate p. 12)*	1-3″ rounded clusters of many slim, rose-purple, 2-lipped tube flowers 1-1/2″ long; each with 2 protruding stamens. Leaves opposite, toothed, fragrant. Square stems.

Curving flowers are crowded into a head or crown at top of stem. Each flower has 2 lips; 2 stamens are attached to the upper lip and protrude conspicuously; the lower lip is 3-lobed and spreading. Leafy, green bracts form a cup for the flower head. Leaves are bright green, ovate, pointed, and have the characteristic mint fragrance. The stems are 1 to 2-1/2′ tall, and are usually unbranched but bunched together on the rootstalk. The entire plant is finely hairy. It grows abundantly along roadsides and in gulches, Plains-Montane. *Monarda fistulosa,* or *menthaefolia,* Mint Family.

NOTES. Menthaefolia means mint-leaved. The leaves of this plant are used for tea, for flavoring, and as a vegetable. Horsemint contains the antiseptic drug, thymol. Bees and humming birds visit the flowers. Horses do not care for horsemint but other livestock and big game eat it.

PARRY PRIMROSE *(p. 37)* *(color plate p. 12)*	5 petals. 2″ loose cluster of brilliant 1/2″ saucer flowers. Yellow centers like eyes. Leaves basal, large, entire. In wet places. Plant 6-16″.

Flowers are a striking bright rose to purplish-red color. The blossoms are borne on long pedicels at the tip of a stout, dark stem, and are among the largest alpine flowers in this region. Sometimes they are nodding. Leaves are long, smooth, thick and deep green. Plant grows in the edge of water, and has a rather disagreeable odor. Subalpine-Alpine. *Primula parryi,* Primrose Family.

ROCKY MOUNTAIN BEE PLANT *(p. 37)* *(color plate p. 13)*	4 separated petals. 2″ cluster of 3/4″ pink flowers; stamens protrude twice the length of petals. Leaves alternate, narrow, and <u>have 3 fingers</u>. Narrow, hanging pods.

Petals are pink to reddish-lavender—rarely white. Pods hang on long, slender stalks. Both flowers and leaves have a rather disagreeable odor. The lower leaves have long petioles; upper ones may be sessile. Plant is smooth branched, and 1-3′ tall. It grows along roadsides and on overgrazed land, Plains-Foothills. *Cleome serrulata,* Caper Family.

NOTES. Because the flowers secrete nectar generously, they provide excellent "bee pasture." Despite the plant's unpleasant odor, Indians boiled and ate both flowers and leaves. Bee Plant is related to the capers used in salads.

PIPSISSIWA or Princes-pine *(p. 37)*	5 petals. 1-1/2″ loose cluster of 1/2″ saucer flowers; prominent greenish pistil. Shiny, stiff, toothed leaves in rows around lower part of stem.

Pink or rose-colored waxy petals surround a conspicuous pistil and 10 hairy stamens that look like little claws. Buds are round and pink. The leathery leaves are evergreen. A rather woody stem 3-6″ tall is circled by rows of leaves. Rising 2-6″ above the leaves is the cluster of flowers. The plant grows in moist evergreen forests or shady bogs. Montane-Subalpine. Colorado and Utah north. *Chimaphila unbellata,* Heath Family.

WILD VERBENA	5 petals open out from a tube. Rose-purple flowers in showy clusters. Leaves opposite, deeply cut. 6-16″ stems decumbent-ascending.

Stems are branched. Plains-Foothills; Okla., Colo., Tex., and Ariz. *Verbena ambrosifolia,* Verbena Family.

RED CLOVER	1-2″ round cluster of tiny pea flowers
(p. 37)	(see Key Terms). <u>Green leaves just</u>
(color plate p. 11)	<u>below head</u>. Clover leaves have 3
	leaflets with <u>light markings</u>. Erect
	plant.

The dense flower clusters may be rose-color to deep red, or sometimes lilac. The leaflets almost always bear more or less distinct white, V-shaped patterns. Plant has several hairy, leafy stems 4-20″ tall, and is common Jun-Sep; Foothills-Montane. *Trifolium pratense,* Pea Family.

NOTE. There are many species of clover throughout the world. They are among our most valuable forage plants because of the nutrition in their high protein content. They are an important food for large birds and deer, elk and bears. Some species were eaten by Indians. A tea is made from Red Clover.

SUBALPINE VALERIAN	5 petals. <u>Flat cluster</u> of tiny pinkish
(p. 38)	flowers; stamens protrude. Leaves
	basal and opposite. Stem leaves
	usually have thumblike lobes. Erect
	plant.

The little pink to whitish flowers are in dense clusters. Basal leaves are entire; the pointed stem leaves—2 to 4 pairs—often have 2 or more distinctive lobes, like thumbs. The plant is smooth, 1-2′ tall, and its root has a strong, disagreeable odor which cats like. It grows in shady, moist ground, Montane-Subalpine. Found from Wyo. to New Mex. and Ariz. *Valeriana capitata,* or *acutiloba,* Valerian Family.

QUEENS-CROWN	5 tiny, <u>pointed, erect petals</u>. Cluster
or Rose-crown	1-1/2″ long of pink flowers at stem
(p. 38)	tip, including some in top axils.
(color plate p. 14)	<u>Leaves alternate, fleshy.</u> Several leafy
	stems. Wet places.

Flowers are very pale pink to rose-color in a crowded cluster. Leaves are gray-green and fleshy (plump) but flattened. The strong, densely leafy stems are 6-14″ tall. These plants commonly grow in wet places; they like to have their feet in the water! The sedums color brilliantly in autumn, adding beauty to the timberline regions. Subalpine. Mont. to New Mex. *Sedum rhodanthum,* Stonecrop Family.

KINGS-CROWN
(p. 38)

One flat, dense cluster 1″ wide, of tiny, <u>dark red flowers</u>. Conspicuous stamens. Leaves alternate and <u>fleshy</u>. Usually a single stem 2-10″ high.

Flowers are maroon or very dark red; may rarely be greenish or tinged with orange. The small leaves are close together and fleshy (nearly circular in cross-section, not flat). Plant grows on wet tundra and in damp places among rocks. Subalpine-Alpine. In late summer, it often turns a brilliant red. *Sedum rosea ssp. integrifolium,* Stonecrop Family.

NOTES. Most members of this family are succulent (fleshy) herbs. Many are edible and are eaten as vegetables and salads in Europe and Asia.

The garden plant, Hen and Chickens, belongs to the Stonecrop Family.

COLLOMIA
(p. 38)

5 petals; dense cluster of tiny pinkish <u>trumpet flowers among leafy bracts</u>. Leaves entire, usually alternate. Stem 2-12″, often on sandy soil.

Little pink or lavender (sometimes reddish-purple) trumpets are bunched at the top of a stem and interspersed with long, slender bracts. The leaves, narrow and pointed, generally turn upwards. The usually unbranched stem grows on disturbed ground along roadsides. Plains-Montane. *Collomia linearis,* Phlox Family.

TUFTED LOCO
(p. 38)

Rose-purple cluster of 1 to 4 pea flowers with a <u>sharp beak</u>. Hairy calyx becomes inflated, covering seeds. <u>5 to 9 gray leaflets</u>. Plant 1-4″ high.

Both calyx and leaflets are hairy. Plant is low, silvery and tufted. When the seeds are forming, the calyx, enclosing them, becomes inflated and it usually turns red, so the little plant may sometimes be tri-colored; gray leaves, red calyx, and perhaps a rose-purple flower still blooming. Grows in gravelly soil, Foothills-Montane. Chiefly from central Colo. to southern Wyo. and Nebr. *Oxytropis multiceps,* Pea Family

NODDING ONION
(p. 38)

6 lobes. 1″ <u>drooping cluster</u> of tiny flowers, rose-pink to pale purple. <u>Protruding stamens</u>. Few leaves; basal, grasslike.

Flowers are in clusters of 5 to 30 which face downwards or sideways because the leafless flower stem has a bend near the top. Leaves are shorter than the flower stalk. When bruised, they have a definite onion smell. Plant is 6-20″ tall, and is common on fields and hillsides, May-Sep; Foothills-Subalpine. *Allium cernuum,* Lily Family. "Cernuum" means nodding.

WILD ONION or Geyers Onion *(p. 38)*	6 lobes <u>pointing up</u>. 1″ cluster of tiny pinkish flowers. <u>3 or more grass-like leaves.</u>

Flowers are pink to light purple—rarely white—in a little umbrella-like cluster. Tips of the inner flower segments are erect or nearly so. The leaves, if crushed, smell like onions. Flower stalk is 1 foot or less; is dwarfed at high altitude. Plant sometimes intergrades with the usually white Sand Onion. May-Sep; Foothills-Timberline. *Allium geyeri,* Lily Family.

NOTES. When not blooming, the onion resembles the highly poisonous Death Camas, the main distinction being the smell of the onion. The flowers of the two plants are very different.

The characteristic odor and taste of onions is caused by the presence of sulphur compounds in the plant.

PINK PUSSYTOES *(p. 38)*	3/4″ dense cluster of flowers like tiny pink balls. No rays or petals. Silvery mat, stem and leaves. Basal leaves narrow at base. Plant has runners.

Pussytoes have disk flowers only. They are pink or rose and look like fuzzy, little balls packed tightly together. The color is due to the red or bright pink papery bracts around the tiny white flowers which are less than 1/4″ long. Leaves are silvery and spoon-shaped. Those on the stem are very small. The plant forms silvery mats from which rise silvery flower stems 4-16″ tall. It is abundant in slightly moist locations; Colorado to Alaska. Foothills-Subalpine. *Antennaria rosea,* Composite Family.

CLOVER *(p. 38)*	Various-sized clusters of small pea flowers (see Key Terms). Leaves have 3 leaflets. 8 species follow.

Four clovers are common in high altitudes—around 9,500 to 13,000 feet. They are small, tufted plants with all leaves basal (except Parry Clover), and they are a favorite food of deer and elk.

RED/HEAD

1. **WHIPROOT CLOVER or ALPINE CLOVER**—Flowers are two-toned, usually creamy-yellow with pink or purple. A compact head of numerous flowers tops a very short, leafless stem. The leaflets are entire, often folded, hairy, and pointed—sometimes almost spine-tipped. Plant is 2-6″ high and often forms a mat. Wyo. and Utah south. *Trifolium dasyphyllum.* Pea Family. *(p. 38)*
2. **DEER CLOVER or DWARF CLOVER**—Flowers are pink or rose, turning brown with age. On each tiny, leafless stem is a loose head of not more than 3 pea flowers. The little leaflets, like most clover leaves, are usually toothed. Plant forms a small mat 1 or 2″ high. Mont. to New Mex. *Trifolium nanum.*
3. **PARRY CLOVER or ROSE CLOVER**—Pea Family. Flowers are rosy-pink or rose-purple and very fragrant. At the base of the compact head are blue-veined, papery bracts that look withered. Leaves are mostly basal with finely-toothed leaflets. Plant, 3-6″ high, may or may not form a mat. Wyo. and Utah south. *Trifolium parryi.*
4. **BRANDEGEE CLOVER**—Looks very much like Parry Clover but: It has no bracts or else extremely small ones and the large, purple flowers bend downwards soon after opening. All leaves basal. Grows in Colo. and New Mex. *Trifolium brandegei.*

Four common clovers are found mostly below 9,500 feet (except Rydberg Clover). Leaves are alternate.

1. **RYDBERG CLOVER**—6.000 to 11,000 feet. Individual flowers in the head are 1/2 to 3/4″ long, are white to pink, and droop when aging. Leaves are both alternate and basal. Leaflet veins end in sharp little teeth. Stems may be erect or ascending. *Trifolium longipes.* *(p. 38)*
2. **FENDLER CLOVER**—Individual flowers, 1/3 to 1/2″, are white to pink. Upper leaflets are larger than the lower. Stems are erect and slightly grooved. *Trifolium fendleri.*
3. **ALSIKE CLOVER**—Individual flowers are about 1/4″ long, are pink to white, droop when aging. Stems erect or ascending. Each tiny calyx tube is white with narrow green teeth (hard to see this without a lens). *Trifolium hybridum.*
4. **STRAWBERRY CLOVER**—Flowers 1/4″. Always pink and always creeping along ground. Chiefly on the plains. *Trifolium fragiferum,* Pea Family.

NOTES. The genus name, *Trifolium,* means 3 leaves, and these mountain clovers typically have 3 leaflets. The author has never found a 4-leaf clover. May you have better luck!
   Clover leaflets fold up and "sleep" at night.

RED/HEAD

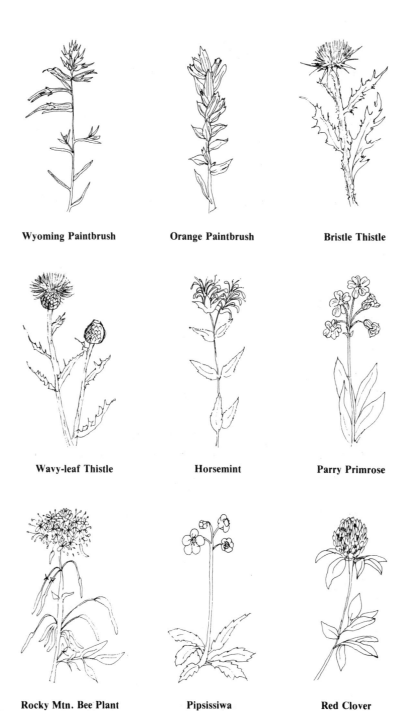

Wyoming Paintbrush　　　**Orange Paintbrush**　　　**Bristle Thistle**

Wavy-leaf Thistle　　　**Horsemint**　　　**Parry Primrose**

Rocky Mtn. Bee Plant　　　**Pipsissiwa**　　　**Red Clover**

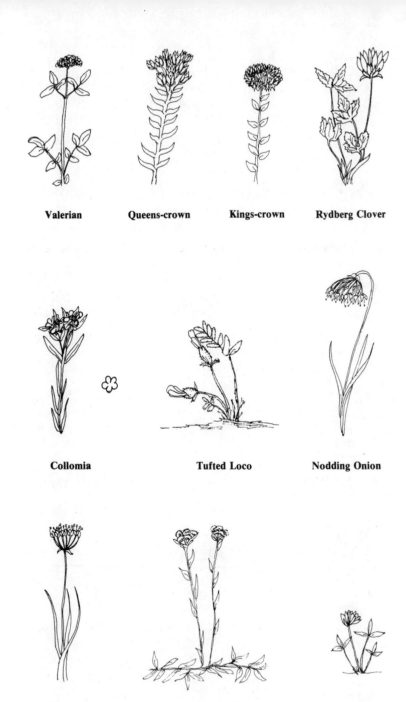

Valerian   Queens-crown   Kings-crown   Rydberg Clover

Collomia   Tufted Loco   Nodding Onion

Wild Onion   Pink Pussytoes   Whiproot Clover

WESTERN WOOD-LILY
(p. 44)
(color plate p. 14)

> Please protect!
> Orange-red trumpet flower 2-4″ deep with dark spots. 6 lobes. Purple stamens. Upper leaves whorled (in rows).

If you should be so fortunate as to find one of these, please protect it carefully. It is very rare. Once fairly common, it has been brought almost to extinction by being picked.

Flower is a brilliant red-orange color and is shaped like a spreading trumpet. It is usually solitary. Its 6 petals and sepals are all alike and are dotted with purple. The narrow, upper leaves are in whorls or rows around the stem; the lower leaves are alternate. Plant is erect, 1-2′ tall, and unbranched. It grows in moist, woodsy places from Mont. to New Mex. in July. *Lilium philadelphicum,* Lily Family.

BITTER-ROOT
(p. 45)

> 12 to 18 pointed petals. Pink to rose colored flower 2-3″ wide. Numerous sepals and stamens. Narrow basal leaves or may appear leafless. Rocky places. Plant usually under 3″.

Each short stem bears a single beautiful, showy blossom with many narrow petals and 4 to 8 sepals. Leaves, 1-2″ long, are bright green and fleshy. They come out early but generally wither before the blooming period starts. Plant grows on stony or gravelly flats, Apr-Jun; Montane. It is rare in Wyo. and Colo. but grows abundantly farther north and west, especially in Mont; also in the Grand Canyon area of Ariz. *Lewisia rediviva,* Purslane Family.

NOTES. Bitter-root is the Montana state flower. The Bitter-root Mtns., River, and Valley in Montana were all named for this plant.
   A dried, withered specimen of this was brought back to Washington, D.C. by members of the Lewis and Clark Expedition in 1806. Many months later, it was revived and planted. When it blossomed, it was named Lewisia for the leader of the Expedition. "Rediviva" means "to live again."

BOUNCING BET
or Soapwort
(p. 45)

> 5 widely separated petals. Clusters of 1-1/4″ pinkish flowers with a 1″ tube. Leaves opposite, entire. Sturdy 1 to 3 foot stems.

Pale pink to lavender or white petals are rounded, notched, and sometimes droop half-way down the light green calyx tube. The stamens are prominent and flowers are usually numerous. The lance-shaped, pointed leaves produce a lather when crushed and rubbed under water. Stems are woody and grow in clumps, often at the mouth of canyons. Jul-Sep; Plains-Foothills. In Colo. and New Mex. *Saponaria officinalis,* Pink Family.

WILD GERANIUM or Cranesbill, or Fremont Geranium *(p. 45)* *(color plate p. 12)*	5 veined, separated petals. 1-1/2″ pink-lavender flowers; usually flat. Showy stamens. Leaves are deeply, palmately lobed. Hairy. Several to many stems.

Flowers are very pale pink to rose and each broad petal is veined with purple. Petal tips are rounded and sometimes notched. Plant is 6-20″ tall and may become quite bushy. It is found on dry ground around rocks or in pine forests, Wyo., Colo., New Mex. and Ariz. Foothills-Montane. *Geranium fremontii,* Geranium Family.

PARRY GERANIUM—grows from Wyo. and Utah south; has rose-purple flowers and rather sticky leaves and stems. *Geranium parryi.*

STICKY GERANIUM—has many rose-purple flowers, is very sticky, and grows Foothills-Montane, from Colo. thru the northern Rockies. *Geranium viscosissimum.*

NOTES. The narrow seed pod, about 1″ long, resembles a crane's bill. The word, geranium, is derived from a Greek word, geranos, meaning "crane."

Geraniums are a major food item for deer, elk, moose, and bears. This genus, geranium, and a related genus, pelargonium (which includes the house-hold plants called "geraniums"), furnish various perfumes.

PINCUSHION CACTUS or Mountain Ball Cactus *(p.45)*	1-1/4″ flower has many bright rosy petals and many sepals and stamens. One large pistil. Low, ball-shaped, prickly plant, radiating spines. No leaves.

The brilliant, pointed, rosy-pink, satiny petals bear a rose fragrance. The pistil, with several stigmas, rises from a yellow nest in the base of the rosy cup. One or more flowers crown the prickly ball that seems to have barely emerged from the ground. This ball is called a stem, and in these cacti, it takes over the functions of leaves. It is slightly flattened, is 1-1/2 to 6″ in diameter and is covered with stout spines. It grows on dry ground and in grassy openings of pine forests.

Foothills-Montane. *Pediocactus,* or *Echinocactus, simpsonii,* Cactus Family.

NOTE. This is an endangered species. In Arizona, the collecting of this and other cacti is prohibited by law. Similar legislation is needed throughout the Rocky Mountain region to protect flowers that are steadily becoming more rare.

FIELD BINDWEED (See White/Saucer)	1″ pink trumpet flower with 5 petals joined, and pink-striped on back. <u>Leaves have 2 lobes at base.</u> Trailing plant.

PACIFIC ANEMONE or Red Anemone or Globe Anemone *(p. 45)*	4 to 9 "petals." <u>One cup-shaped 1″ flower tops each slender stem.</u> <u>Leaves cut into narrow parts.</u> Hairy plant under 1 ft. Seed pods like thimbles.

Flower is usually deep red but may be pink or yellowish. Anemones do not have true petals but the showy sepals look just like petals. The leaves are all near the base of the plant but around the stem perhaps half-way up is a circle or collar of large bracts that look just like leaves, and that originally enclosed the bud but were left below as the flower developed and pushed up. Both leaves and bracts are deeply cleft into narrow segments and both have petioles. This silky-hairy plant grows in open woods and on grassy slopes. Montane-Alpine, *Anemone multifida,* ssp. *globosa.* Buttercup Fam.

FAIRY PRIMROSE *(p. 45)*	5 bright rose-purplish petals surround <u>a yellow eye center.</u> Basal, oblong leaves. 1-3″ high. Alpine.

The fragrant petals are often notched. Leaves form a basal rosette 2-8″ wide. Plant usually grows in exposed locations; occasionally it hides in rocky nooks. The stems are often in clusters and each little stem bears one flower. Southern central Rocky Mtns. *Primula angustifolia,* Primrose Family.

NOTE. Despite the similarity in names, the Primrose Family and the Evening-primrose Family are quite different. For example: all members of the Evening-primrose Family in our area have 4 petals; the flowers of the Primrose Family have 5.

COPPER MALLOW (See Red/Stalk)	5 petals. <u>Salmon-colored</u> saucer flowers Orange stamens. Leaves alternate, <u>gray, divided.</u> Dry places. 4-10″.

41

MOUNTAIN PHLOX (See White/Saucer)	Flat flowers with 5 pink petals. Stamens are inside the slender 1/2″ tube with a tiny opening at top. Loose mat 2-4″ high with needle-like leaves.
SPRING-BEAUTY *(p. 46)*	5 veined petals; 1/2″ pale pinkish flower; has only 2 sepals. Leaves opposite, entire. Delicate plant 2-6″ high.

Flowers are white to pink with veins of deeper pink. They close at sunset and on cloudy days. There is one pair of lance-shaped, pointed leaves on the stem and in some cases, a third leaf at the base. The plant likes moist ground; and is frequently found under scrub oaks. Apr-Jul; Foothills-Subalpine. Big game and rodents feed on this plant. *Claytonia lanceolata and rosea,* Purslane Family.

WATER SPRING-BEAUTY—or **INDIAN LETTUCE** is closely related to the preceding and the flower, pink or white, looks just the same, with only 2 sepals. Water Spring-beauty, however, usually has 2 or more pairs of leaves, broader at the end, and it is a floating or creeping plant in or beside water. Sends out runners as strawberries do. *Montia chamissoi,* Purslane Family.

SWAMP LAUREL or Bog Laurel *(p. 46)*	5 crinkled petals. Many 1/2″ pink or rose flowers. Leaves opposite, narrow, entire, evergreen, white below. Plant 4-8″, or 18″.

Flowers are shallow or deep saucers. Leaves are leathery, 1/2 to 1″ long and narrow, often appearing even narrower because their edges may roll under against the white lower side. In Colorado, this woody plant is 4-8″ high. At timberline it may appear to be almost creeping. From Wyoming north, it grows at lower altitudes and becomes a low shrub up to 18″. Is found on peaty soil in very wet, cold places. Subalpine. *Kalmia polifolia,* Heath Family.

STORKSBILL or Filaree *(p. 46)*	5 petals. 3/8″ delicate flower. Leaves fernlike; often flat on ground. Bird-bill pods may turn upward. Plant 1-10″.

This is one of the first flowers to appear in spring. Little pink to lavender or reddish-purple blossoms are borne on leafless, hairy stalks. The leaves are very finely cut and usually some of them lie on the ground. Plant is generally low and sprawling. The seed pods, about 1″ long, resemble a stork's bill. Apr-Jul; Plains-Foothills. This was introduced to the United States from Europe and being very

RED/SAUCER

adaptable, it crowds out many native plants. It does, however, provide valuable forage. *Erodium cicutarium,* Geranium Family.

MOSS CAMPION	5 petals widely separated and oblong.
or Cushion Pink	1/4″ flat, pink flowers; 1/4″ striped
(p. 46)	calyx. Mossy cushion 1/2 to 3″ high. Alpine.

Flowers are bright pink to rose-color—rarely white. Leaves are tiny and pointed. The little green cushion, 3-12″ wide, is set with pink stars which may be so thick as to nearly cover the plant. *Silene acaulis,* Pink Family.

NOTES. This alpine flower is very common on exposed rocky places, and it grows on cold, windy mountain ridges throughout the Northern Hemisphere, including the Scottish highlands and the peaks of the Alps.
 Carnations and garden pinks also belong to the Pink Family.

| **WILLOW-HERB** | 4 petals. Small cup-like flowers. |
| *(p. 46)* | Leaves small, usually opposite. Branches, if any, are often erect. Usually in wet places. 4-24″. |

The little lavender, pink or white cups (sometimes rose or purple) are rarely wide open. Petals may be notched. The erect pods, 1/2 to 2-1/2″ long, often turn up and may be touched with red. Willowherb is common and wide-spread. Plains-Subalpine. One small alpine species (E. alpinum) has an S-shaped stem. Another species grows on dry soil. *Epilobium hornemanni, paniculatum,* and others, Evening-Primrose Family.

NOTES. Willow-herb might be confused with Love Gentian, but Love Gentian petals spread out from a small, open tube with fringe in the throat. Willow-herb has a little cup flower on top of a slender pod (ovary) which, when ripe, will split open with its 4 sides curling out to release 4 tiny seeds, each bearing a tuft of small white hairs at its tip, like willow seeds; hence the name, "willow-herb."
 The botanical name, *epilobium,* comes from Greek words meaning, "Upon the pod."

DRUMMOND	4 petals. Small, flat flower. Few waxy
ROCK-CRESS	alternate leaves, wider at base and
(p. 46)	clasping stem with "ears." Pods like big needles stand straight up 1-1/2 to 4″ beside the stem.

There are usually 1 to 3 pale pink, white, or lavender flowers at the top of the stem. Although common, Rock-cress is inconspicuous. A few leaves, narrow and bluish, with or without teeth, are scattered sparsely along the stem. The one to several stems are erect, slender but stout, and 3-30″ tall, with no branches and no hair. Plains-Alpine. *Arabis drummondi,* Mustard Family.

HAIRY ROCK-CRESS—*Arabis hirsuta,* has erect pods and is rather hairy. Other species of Rock-cress are distinguished chiefly by whether the pods spread out, or hang down.

NOTE. In some cases Rock-cress might be confused with Willow-herb. The following may help:

Rock-cress	Willow-herb
Is usually found in dry places. Leaves are always alternate. Flowers are nearly always flat. Leaves usually clasp stem with little "ears."	Usually grows in wet places. Leaves are—usually—opposite. Flowers are more or less cup-shaped. Leaf bases seldom have ears.

MICROSTERIS (See White/Saucer)	5 notched petals. Tiny, flat flowers. Lower leaves opposite. Tiny plant easily overlooked.

Western Wood-lily

Bitter-root

Bouncing Bet

Wild Geranium

Pincushion Cactus

Pacific Anemone

Fairy Primrose

Spring-beauty

Swamp Laurel

Storksbill

Moss Campion

Willow-herb

Drummond Rock-cress

PINK PLUMES
or Prairie Smoke
(p. 50)
(color plate p. 11)

5 petals protrude thru the sides of a ball-like flower. The flowers—1/2 to 1-1/2"—usually hang in sets of 3. Fern-like leaves. Silky seed plumes.

Flowers are often a dusty-rose color that may shade into deep pink or purple. 5 sepals overlap, forming a rounded ball; the petals, which are smaller and paler, protrude from the sides of the ball and may extend horizontally or even curl upwards. The styles (tip of pistil) are very long and after blooming they develop into showy, pink, silky plumes of feathery seed tails. Leaves, mainly basal, are 2-8" long with 9 to 19 pinnate leaflets, the smallest ones near the base. This is one of the first plants to send up green leaves after the snow melts in spring. It is 6-24" tall and rather hairy. Apr-Sep; Foothills-Subalpine. *Geum triflorum,* or *Sieversia ciliata,* Rose Family.

NOTE. Indians made a tea from the roots of Pink Plumes.

SHOOTING-STAR
(p. 50)
(color plate p. 14)

1" dart-shaped flowers. 5 rose-pink petals with yellow bases flare back from the dark-colored dart. Leaves basal and entire. In wet places.

Flowers are unique because they are shaped like darts. The narrow, bright pink petals flare outward and backward. At their base, the petals unite in a short yellow tube from which protrude 5 dark anthers joined in a straight, sharp beak about 1/4" long—the point of the dart. These darts usually point downwards, and several flowers may nod from the top of a slender, fleshy stem. Leaves are smooth, deep green, and lance-shaped. Plant is 8-16" tall and is abundant along stream banks and in wet meadows. Foothills-Subalpine. *Dodocatheon pulchellum,* Primrose Family.

FAIRY-SLIPPER
(p. 50)
(color plate p. 11)

Please Protect! 1" flower is like a tiny pink moccasin. Wide lower petal forms toe with yellow hairs at opening, and purple lines. Only 1 leaf—at base.

This is an orchid; one of the prettiest in this region. Please protect it because, although not so rare as its larger cousin, the Yellow Lady's-Slipper, its numbers have been greatly reduced by picking. The single, pink or rose-colored flower has 3 sepals. The lowest (and much the largest) petal is called the lip and is in the form of a pink sac with dots and yellow hairs, and purple lines inside. This lip gives the appearance of a delicate, beautiful little slipper. There is a bend in the

47

RED/MISC.

flower stem near its top. Although the stem is sheathed, there is only one leaf. This is broad, entire, and conspicuously veined. The single stem is 3-8″ high and is usually found in damp, shady places among evergreens, growing on completely buried, largely disintegrated logs. Foothills-Subalpine. *Calypso bulbosa,* Orchid Family.

NOTE. Fairy-slipper was named Calypso for the island nymph of Greek legends.

BROOMRAPE	2-lipped tube flower, 1″ long, variable in color. Scale-like leaves. <u>No green on plant</u>. 6″ tall or less.

Flowers may be pinkish or brownish or purplish or yellow. They rise on thick stalks along or above the fleshy, usually pinkish-brown, main stem. This is a parasite on sagebrush and eriogonum. Plains-Montane. *Orobanche fasciculata,* Broomrape Family.

WESTERN RED COLUMBINE *(p. 50)*	1″ hanging, spurred flower with 5 red sepals; and 5 yellowish petals extending into 5 straight, red spurs. Delicate, lobed leaflets.

The petals and sepals lie close together and since the flower hangs down, the spurs point upward. Leaves are mostly basal, on long stalks and usually have 3 leaflets with rounded lobes that may be bluish-green below. Plant 4-16″ high, prefers moist, wooded places west of the Continental Divide. Montane zone. Colo., Utah and New Mex. *Aquilegia elegantula,* Buttercup Family.

SPREADING DOGBANE (See Red/Stalk)	Small, hanging clusters of 1/3″ pink bellflowers; red veining inside. Leaves opposite, shiny above; may or may not droop. <u>Erect plant 8-24″</u>.

BLUEBERRY or Grouseberry or Bilberry or Whortleberry *(p. 50)*	Tiny, pink, urn-shaped flowers usually hidden under alternate, <u>toothed, thin leaves, 1/4 to 1″</u>. Delicate ground cover 2-10″ high under evergreen forests.

Flowers are pink or white, and single or in small clusters. Although Blueberry is so low and delicate that it looks like a dainty, spreading plant, it is actually a creeping shrub and often forms a lacy carpet for miles under evergreen trees. The berries are red or dark blue or blue-black, according to the species, and are well-liked by many birds and animals. Montane-Alpine. *Vaccinium scoparium, caespitosum* and *myrtillus, Heath Family.*

| **TWIN-FLOWER** *(p. 50)* | 1 pair of tiny pinkish bell-flowers on each <u>erect, thread-like stem</u>. Leaves <u>opposite, thin, toothed</u>. Creeping plant in damp woods. |

Leafless flower stems, 2-4" high, each bear one pair of dainty little pink and white bells, which are sweetly fragrant. The inner base of the 5 petals is pink and hairy. Leaves are rounded, 1/4 to 1/2" wide, evergreen, and glossy, with scalloped edges. These delicate, trailing stems grow in damp, evergreen forests. Montane-Subalpine. *Linnaea borealis,* Honeysuckle Family.

NOTE. Because it was one of his favorite flowers, Twin-flower was named Linnaea in honor of the famous Swedish botanist, Carolus Linnaeus (died 1778), the man who was largely responsible for the binomial system of naming plants and animals. This system assigns a generic (genus) and a specific (species) name to a plant and these two Latin words form the botanical name; the first word—a noun—denotes the genus to which it belongs, and the second—a descriptive adjective—applies only to a smaller, restricted group or species. Although the same species may be known locally by various names in different parts of the country, the botanical name is recognized throughout the world as denoting that particular group.

| **KINNIKINNIK** (See White/Misc.) | 1/4" pink and white jug-like flowers hanging among leaves, on <u>low mat</u> in dry woods. Leaves <u>alternate, entire, shiny, leathery</u>. |

Pink Plumes

Shooting-star

Fairy-slipper

Western Red Columbine

Blueberry

Twin-flower

Pearly Everlasting
(p. 85)

Miner's Candle
(p. 71)

Brook-cress
(p. 82)

Cow Parsnip
(p. 79)

Yarrow
(p. 83)

Canada Violet
(p. 97)

White Marsh-marigold
(p. 94)

Rocky Mtn. Thimbleberry
(p. 59)

52

Chickweed
(p. 98)

Wood-nymph
(p. 95)

Alpine Anemone
or
Narcissus Anemone
(p. 93)

Alpine Sandwort
(p. 98)

Chokecherries
(p. 62)

Prickly Poppy
(p. 91)

Daisy
(p. 56)

Mariposa-lily
(p. 92)

OX-EYE DAISY (p. 57)	1-1/2 to 3″ white flower, usually one on each long stem. Yellow center. Leaves alternate, narrow, <u>sharply, unevenly toothed</u>. Plant 1 to 2-1/2′.

The rays, 1/4″ wide or more, are notched at tip and the green bracts form a saucer-shaped involucre. The deep green leaves are 1-6″ long; upper ones are mostly sessile. Plant was introduced from Europe; is common along roadsides and in fields and meadows; Plains-Montane. *Chrysanthemum leucanthemum or Leucanthemum vulgaris,* Composite Family.

EASTER DAISY (p. 58)	1-2″ flowers very low. Have greenish-yellow center and grooved, white rays. Leaves ashy-gray, grasslike. <u>No plant stem</u>—flowers and leaves rise from root crown at ground level.

Flower nestles among the leaves close to the ground. There are about 30 wide, white (or sometimes pinkish) rays. Easter Daisy is one of the earliest spring flowers in this region. Plant is tufted and grows on sunny, sandy slopes, Mar-Jun; Foothills-Montane. Because it is so low and compact and usually occurs as an isolated plant, it may easily be overlooked. *Townsendia hookeri and exscapa,* Composite Family.

SHOWY TOWNSENDIA (See Red/Daisy Shape)	Flower has greenish-yellow center. Rays grooved. Leaves gray, grasslike. <u>Has one to several 2-8″ stems</u> bearing leaves and flowers.

WHITE MARSH-MARIGOLD (See White/Saucer)	1-1/2″ saucer flowers with 5 to 15 rounded "petals." Many crowded, yellow stamens. Bluish buds. <u>Leaves basal, rounded, 3-8″ wide</u>. In wet places.

This is one of the few Saucer flowers that might be mistaken for a Daisy type because its stamens and pistils are packed so closely in the center.

BLACK-HEADED DAISY (p. 58)	1-1/4″ flower has white rays, a yellow center and <u>dark, soft-woolly bracts</u>. Spoon-shaped, entire leaves; smaller ones on stem. <u>Plant 2-6″</u>.

Each stem has a single flower with purplish-black, woolly bracts.

The plant grows near melting snow. Subalpine-Alpine. Found from Wyo. and Utah to New Mex. *Erigeron melanocephalus,* Composite Family.

COULTER DAISY or Coulter Erigeron *(p. 58)*	Flower, 3/4 to 1-1/2″, has many rays, a yellow center and <u>dark-hairy bracts</u>. Upper leaves may clasp stem. <u>Plant 10-20″ tall</u>.

There is—usually—just one head at the top of the stem, with 50 to 100 white rays. The long hairs on the bracts are thick and look dark because of black "crosswalls" near their bases. The lower leaves are petioled. Plant has one to several hairy, leafy stems. It prefers damp soil and grows chiefly on the Western Slope, Jul-Sep; Montane-Subalpine. *Erigeron coulteri,* Composite Family.

SPREADING DAISY (See Blue/Daisy Shape)	3/4″ flower has very narrow rays and a yellow center. Narrow leaves, lobed or entire. <u>Many spreading stems</u>. Hairy. <u>Stem hairs spread outwards</u>.

WHIPLASH DAISY or Whiplash Erigeron (er IJ er on) *(p. 58)*	1/2″ single flower, yellow center, <u>narrow</u> white rays, <u>pink on back</u>. <u>Pink buds droop</u>. Leaves entire. May have runners.

This is one of the most common of the many species of daisies found in this region. It is 3-10″ tall and likes moist soil. From June on, it sends out trailing, leafy runners which grow roots at the tips as strawberry plants do. Apr-Aug; Plains-Subalpine. *Erigeron Flagellaris,* Composite Family.

NOTE. The name, "Daisy" is derived from Day's Eye, referring to the resemblance of the flower's yellow center and its rays, to the sun and its rays.

For distinctions between Daisies and Asters, see Key Terms or Glossary.

WHITE ASTERS *(p. 58)*	1/2 to 3/4″ flowers; white rays, yellow centers, <u>aster bracts</u>. Flowers usually numerous. Narrow leaves. Branched plants. 3 common species follow:

1. **PORTER ASTER**—Flowers 1/2 to 3/4″. As the orange-yellow centers age, they <u>turn brown or dark red</u>. The bracts are green.

Leaves, 1/2 to 4″ long, have no hair except sometimes along the edge. Plant is 6-18″ tall and non-hairy. This is the most common white aster of the mountains, growing on open sunny slopes and meadows. Foothills-Subalpine but chiefly in the Montane zone; Jul-Sep. Colo. and New Mex. *Aster porteri,* Composite Family.

2. **ROUGH WHITE ASTER**—The 1/2″ flowers have <u>tiny bristles on the tips of the bracts.</u> The leaves, 1/4 to 2″ long, are stiff, linear, rough-hairy, and have <u>tiny bristles on their tips.</u> The rough-hairy stems are 8-20″ tall, the hairs spread out; do not rest against the stem. Grows along roadsides and on dry, sandy places, Plains-Foothills; Jul-Sep. *Aster falcatus or commutatus,* Composite Family

3. **SAND ASTER**—There is only one 1/4″ flower on each branch but the slender branches are so thick that the flowers seem crowded. Rays are short. Tiny, rigid, entire leaves. Plant is <u>not over 5″ tall; in tufts of numerous, fine, wiry, rather rough-hairy stems.</u> On dry, sandy soil of plains and foothills, Jul-Sep., Wyo. to New Mex. *Aster arenosus or ericoides.*

CUT-LEAF DAISY or Cut-leaf Erigeron *(p. 58)*	One 1/2″ flower on each stem, yellow-button center. Leaves cut, with <u>3-forked ends.</u> Plant 2-6″. Dry places.

Flower has white rays (rarely pink or blue). Leaves are fan-shaped and are divided into 3's two or more times. Plant grows in tufts on dry, stony soil. Foothills-Subalpine. *Erigeron compositus,* Composite Family.

One rather common form of this—**GOLD BUTTONS**—has no ray flowers; just the yellow button. Leaves are the same.

Ox-eye Daisy

Easter Daisy

Black-headed Daisy

Coulter Daisy

Whiplash Daisy

Rough White Aster

Cut-leaf Daisy

THIMBLEBERRY *(p. 65)* *(color plate p. 52)*	5 rounded petals. 2-3″ saucer flowers. Leaves 1-1/2 to 10″, alternate or in clusters; have toothed lobes. 2 species follow.

1. **ROCKY MOUNTAIN THIMBLEBERRY or BOULDER RASPBERRY.** The numerous beautiful blossoms occur singly and look like single, white roses. The 2″ leaves have toothed, mostly rounded lobes. They are bright green above and paler beneath. Shrub, 2-6′ tall, has graceful, arching branches and light brown, shreddy bark.

   The botanical name is misleading. The berries are not delicious; they are insipid. Birds and animals eat them and deer eat the foliage. The shrub is very common in sunny, rocky locations in Colo. and Wyo., chiefly east of the Continental Divide. Foothills-Montane. *Rubus deliciosus,* Rose Family.

2. **THIMBLEBERRY**—Flowers, of shallow cup shape, are in clusters of 2 to 9. Leaves are 3-10″ broad with toothed, pointed lobes. Upright shrub, prefers damp or shady places. Is more common on the Western Slope throughout the Rockies. *Rubus parviflorus.*

LITTLE-LEAF MOCKORANGE or Syringa	4 (or 5) petals. 3/4 to 1-1/2″ flower. 20 or more yellow stamens. Buds green and white. Branches and silvery leaves opposite.

Flowers solitary or in 2's or 3's at ends of branches. Small pale leaves. On rocky slopes, Plains-Foothills, in southern Rockies. Indians used the stems for making arrows. *Philadelphus microphyllus,* Saxifrage Family.

LEWIS MOCKORANGE or SYRINGA—similar to above with 4 petals and opposite leaves and branches but has numerous smaller, fragrant flowers and larger leaves. Dry places in Idaho and Mont. It is the state flower of Idaho. *Philadelphus lewisii.*

FENDLERBUSH—also, is like Mockorange with 4 petals and opposite leaves but the flower has only 8 stamens and the buds are rose-tinged. Colo. and Texas to Ariz. *Fendlera rupicola,* Saxifrage Family.

HAWTHORN (p. 65)	5 petals. Clusters of 3/4" saucer flowers; showy stamens; fragrant. Stout, 1-1/2" sharp thorns. Broad leaves, alternate, doubly toothed. Along creeks and canyons. 2 common species follow.

The conspicuous stamens may be pink, white, rose, or purple. The shrub (or small tree) is 2-16′ tall. The berry-like fruits are called "haws" and are related to apples. Foothills-Montane.

1. **SHINY-LEAVED or RED-STEMMED HAWTHORN**—has shiny leaves and stems, (no hair), and dark red to black haws. Wyo. to New Mex. and Ariz. *Crataegus erythropoda,* Rose Family.
2. **COLORADO or WESTERN HAWTHORN**—has dull, rather hairy leaves, and bright red haws. Found from Canada to Colo. and Ariz. *Crataegus succulenta.* The two species hybridize.

SERVICEBERRY or Juneberry or Shadbush (p. 65)	5 oblong petals, widely separated. Clusters of 3/4" saucer flowers. Showy stamens. 1" roundish leaves, alternate, toothed, and prominently veined in back.

Petals are fragrant and sometimes twisted. Leaves are ovate to round, with tiny teeth along the upper half. Shrub may be small to large. The blue berries are edible and are a favorite food of many animals. Foothills-Subalpine. *Amelanchier alnifolia,* Rose Family.

WILD PLUM (p. 65)	Umbels of creamy-white, fragrant flowers open before or with the leaves. Inside of calyx is woolly. Branches rigid, usually in dense thickets. Bark grayish. Few blunt thorns. Near creeks. Leaves alternate.

5 petals. The outside of the starlike calyx is reddish. The 2-4" leaves are taper-pointed and finely toothed. Shrub is 5-9′ tall, often grows in almost impenetrable thickets, and is found along streams and in moist places, mainly on the eastern side of the Continental Divide; Apr-May; Plains-Foothills. Fruit is yellow or red with a flattened pit. *Prunus americana,* Rose Family.

PIN CHERRY or Bird Cherry *(p. 65)*	5 petals. 1/2″ white flowers in loose umbels of 3 to 7; <u>bloom as leaves un-fold</u>. Leaves alternate, long-pointed, toothed. <u>New bark glossy, brown with white marks</u>. <u>No thorns</u>.

Flowers are little saucers, somewhat fragrant. The bright red, 1/4″ cherries have a large, round seed; birds are fond of them. Leaves are narrow lance-shaped and finely toothed. The bark, except on old trunks, is glossy brown with spots or horizontal markings. Pin Cherry grows in small scattered clumps rather than in dense stands; is seldom over 4′ tall. Found along streams and also on stony hillsides, especially east of the Continental Divide. Foothills-Montane. *Prunus pennsylvanica,* Rose Family.

WAXFLOWER or Jamesia *(p. 65)*	5 <u>waxy-white petals</u>. Clusters of 1/2″ flowers. Buds may be pink-tinged. Leaves <u>opposite</u>, ovate, <u>scalloped, deeply veined</u>, pale below.

Numerous flowers with petals widely separated at the ends. Leaves are dark green above and soft-hairy underneath. In autumn, they turn various shades of red. The larger stems have peeling bark. Waxflower is 2-6′ tall. It is often found in rock crevices or at the base of cliffs; Foothills-Subalpine but is abundant in the montane zone. *Jamesia americana,* Saxifrage Family.

NOTES: This genus was named for Dr. Edwin James who discovered it, and who in 1820 with two companions, made the first ascent of Pikes Peak by white men.

The shrub, Jamesia or Waxflower, is a very ancient species. Impressions of Jamesia leaves have been found in Oligocene deposits in southern Colorado.

WILD RED RASPBERRY *(p. 66)*	5 petals. The saucer flowers are usually hidden under deeply veined leaves. The <u>toothed</u> <u>leaflets are whitish below</u>. <u>Prickly shrub</u> 1-2′ high.

Flowers are not noticeable because they are usually tucked in among the leaves in loose clusters of 2 to 6. Slender sepals are plainly visible between the rounded petals. The alternate leaves have 3 or 5 sharply-toothed leaflets that are gray-hairy or matted white beneath. Shrub has very bristly stems and it grows along roadsides and on rocky slopes; Foothills-Subalpine. *Rubus idaeus or strigosus,* Rose Family.

RED ELDERBERRY
or Red-berried Elder
(p. 66)

5 petals. 3/8″ saucer flowers in large pyramid-shaped heads. Later, bright red berries. Opposite leaves with 5 to 7 toothed leaflets.

The creamy-white flowers are in dense clusters 1-1/2 to 5″ high. The lance-shaped, pointed leaflets are green above; paler below. This variable shrub is 2-8′ tall in this region. It is common, dense, and attractive; usually growing in moist places on north slopes; Foothills-Subalpine. *Sambucus racemosa, ssp. pubens,* Honeysuckle Family.

Two other species very similar to the preceding are: **BLACK ELDERBERRY**—*Sambucus melanocarpa,* with black berries. **BLUE ELDERBERRY**—*Sambucus coerulea,* with flat-topped flower heads, oblong leaflets and bluish berries.

NOTE. Indians ate elderberries fresh or dried, used the flowers as medicine, and made flutes and clappers from the pithy stems.

CHOKECHERRY
(p. 66)
(color plate p. 54)

5 petals, Numerous yellow stamens. Many fragrant saucer flowers in finger-like clusters 2-6″ long. Alternate, pointed leaves. Bark "brown, bitter and blotchy."

The cylinder-like clusters often droop. Petals are white but the stamens usually give the flower a creamy tint. Leaves are rather wide, finely toothed, and pale below. Shrub is upright and—in the Rockies—is 2-15′ tall. There are light spots on the brown bark. It grows along streams and on hill-sides, often in thickets. Plains-Montane. *Prunus virginiana, var. melanocarpa,* Rose Family.

NOTES. The fruit, a single-stoned, black cherry, has a "puckery" taste raw but makes excellent jelly. Indians ate the cherries fresh and dried. They made a green dye from the bark and a red dye from the berries.

Members of the Lewis and Clark expedition, and other early explorers ate the cherries. Bears and birds, including pheasants, like them and the leaves, stems and buds are eaten by mountain goats, elk, deer, and moose.

The seeds, themselves, are poisonous, like peach pits.

Chokecherries are related to apples, apricots, cherries, peaches, pears, plums, blackberries, raspberries and strawberries—also almonds—all of which belong to the Rose Family.

MOUNTAIN-ASH
(p. 66)

| 5-petaled flowers in large, flat clusters. Leaves alternate, with 11 to 15 sharply-toothed leaflets. Moist hillsides. |

The flower clusters may be 2-6″ wide and sometimes have as many as 40 flowers. The pointed leaflets are 1-3″ long. Shrub is stout and beautiful, is 3-12′ tall, and is more common on the West Slope. Foothills-Subalpine. *Sorbus scopulina,* Rose Family.

ROCKY MOUNTAIN NINEBARK
or Colorado Low Ninebark
(p. 66)

| 5 petals. 1/3″ saucer flowers, usually in a tight cluster. Protruding stamens. Leaves alternate; rounded, with 3 to 5 doubly toothed lobes. |

Numerous 1″, umbel-like clusters of flowers, sometimes with a tinge of pink—on the buds, or the stamen tips, or on withering sepals. In autumn, the leaves turn orange or red. Shrub, 1-6′ tall, is often low and spreading. Thin layers of the brown bark are continually shredding off the older stems, leaving several shades of color; hence the name, ninebark. This common species of ninebark, occurs frequently in shady places and on north slopes. Foothills-Montane; From southern Wyo. to Ariz. and New Mex. *Physocarpus monogynus,* Rose Family.

GOOSEBERRY
(p. 66)

| 5 separated petals shorter than the sepals. Small clusters of bell or tube-shaped flowers. Clusters of small lobed leaves. Prickly shrub with sharp spines. 2 species follow. |

1. **WILD GOOSEBERRY**—1 to 4 flowers in a white or pink cluster. The petals open out from the tube and the long sepals are usually reflexed (drooping). Blooms in June. Leaves have 3 to 5 toothed lobes, and they are in small alternate clusters, often very thick along the branches. Shrub is usually under 3 feet with arching stems. Common in moist, shady places; Foothills-Subalpine. Fruit is tart and wine or dark purplish; often tipped with withered flower parts. *Ribes inerme,* Gooseberry Family.

2. **THIN-FLOWERED or TRUMPET GOOSEBERRY**—Much like the preceding but the flowers are pink, white or yellowish, are slightly hairy, have red-tipped stamens, and the sepals are not reflexed. They bloom in April. Shrub is 1-6′ tall, with branches ascending to erect. Found on dry slopes in the southern Rockies. *Ribes leptanthum.*

63

**RED-OSIER
   DOGWOOD**
(p. 66)

| 4 or 5 tiny petals. 1/3″ flowers in 1-2″ flat clusters. Opposite, entire leaves. Red stems 3-6′. Along streams. |

The numerous leaves are 1-4″ long, pointed, and usually ovate. Shrub is common, growing in thickets, generally 3-6′ tall. The branches are smooth and red. Dogwood is easily recognized in winter by the red bark. *Cornus stolonifera,* Dogwood Family.

NOTE. The stems or "osiers" were used by Indians for making baskets. Leaves and inner stems were used by Indians and early settlers as a tobacco substitute. The whitish berries are valuable food for birds and bears. The shrub also provides winter food for rabbits, deer, elk and moose.

**HIGH-BUSH
   CRANBERRY**
or Arrowwood
(p. 66)

| 5 petals. A few clusters of 1/4″ flowers. Leaves opposite, broad, toothed, slightly 3-lobed. This is a straggly shrub. |

Axillary clusters of flowers develop into little red, flattened berries that have been used as a substitute for cranberries. Shrub, 1-6′ tall is straggly with few stems. It grows in moist, shady places. Montane-Subalpine. From Colo. to Canada. *Viburnum edule or pauciflorum,* Honeysuckle Family.

MOUNTAIN-BALM

| 5 small petals, each with a narrow claw. Leaves alternate, oval, leathery, shiny (look varnished) and sweet-scented. |

Dense clusters of small flowers. Leaves evergreen, toothed and 2″ long. Shrub 1-6′, often in patches. Foothills-Montane. From Colo. north. *Ceanothus velutinus,* Buckthorn Family.

MOUNTAIN-SPRAY
or Rock Spirea
(p. 66)

| Profuse sprays of tiny flowers. Leaves small, alternate, non-shiny, wedge-shaped, toothed, pale-hairy below. In rocky canyons. |

Delicate flower clusters are often so numerous as to nearly cover the shrub. White or creamy-white at first, they later turn pink and finally rust color, remaining on the branches all summer and appearing as large, rusty patches on a rocky slope. Leaves are smooth-green above and silky-white beneath. When bruised, they smell like green apples. They resemble Mountain Mahogany leaves but the latter has stipules and its leaves are usually clustered. The shrub is fine-textured with straight stems 3-6' tall. Foothills-Montane. Mountain Spray is related to the cultivated spireas. *Holodiscus dumosus and discolor,* Rose Family.

NEW JERSEY TEA
or Fendler Ceanothus
or Buckbrush
(p. 66)

5 petals. Many 3/16" flowers in clusters. <u>Leaves alternate, short, narrow, entire. Thorny shrub 8-16" high.</u>

The petals, off-white to pink-tinged, are joined and they bloom in delicate, umbel-like clusters; sometimes so thick as to cover the entire shrub. Leaves, about 1/2" long, are silvery on lower side. Shrub is very thorny and grows on dry, rocky slopes in Colo. Utah, Ariz., New Mex. and Texas. Despite the thorns, it is eaten by deer, porcupines and livestock. *Ceanothus fendleri,* Buckthorn Family.

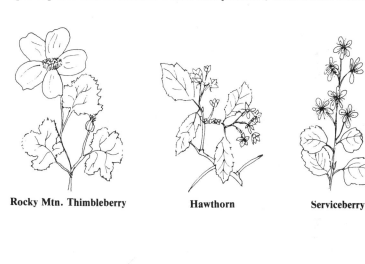

Rocky Mtn. Thimbleberry   **Hawthorn**   **Serviceberry**

Wild Plum   **Pin Cherry**   **Waxflower**

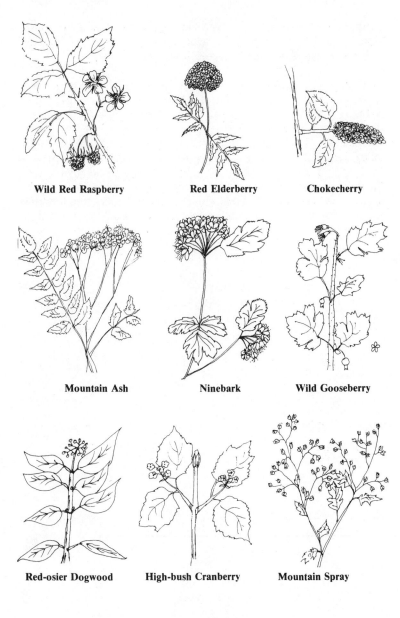

Wild Red Raspberry   Red Elderberry   Chokecherry

Mountain Ash   Ninebark   Wild Gooseberry

Red-osier Dogwood   High-bush Cranberry   Mountain Spray

New Jersey Tea

YUCCA or Soapweed or Spanish Bayonet *(p. 76)*	6 lobes (3 petals and 3 sepals). 2″ bell-flowers hang along a tall, thick, woody spike. Dagger-like leaves 1/2″ wide.*

In daytime the flowers are drooping bells; in the evening they open out like lilies to a width of 3 or 4″. The 3 petals are creamy or greenish-white; the 3 sepals are often mahogany-brown. 6 white stamens surround a green-tipped pistil. The leaves, 10 to 30″ long and about 1/2″ wide, are stiff, spear-like and yellowish-green with a sharp spine at the tip, hence the name—Spanish Bayonet. Thread-like fibers sometimes fray out along the edges. This plant, 1 to 6′ tall, is evergreen and is common on dry, sandy soil. Plains-Foothills, in Colo., New Mex. and Texas. *Yucca glauca,* Lily Family.

NOTES. Yucca pollen is too heavy and sticky to be transferred from flower to flower like the powdery pollen of most other plants, which is carried by wind or by insects that brush against it when they stop to gather flower nectar. Pollination of the yucca is accomplished only by the Pronuba moth, a small, white insect that flies at night. The moth picks up a little ball of yucca pollen and carries it to another yucca flower. Here she pierces the wall of the ovary and deposits an egg inside. Then she climbs up the pistil and places the ball of pollen next to the stigma, which insures fertilization of a yucca ovule. She repeats this process several times. Then when the tiny grubs hatch, food is ready for them in the form of the developing seeds. They eat their way out, leaving a tiny hole in the ripened pod. Neither yucca nor moth could survive without the other.

Yucca has long, tough fibers which the Indians used for making cord, thread, mats, sandals and baskets. They also obtained food from the flowers and fruits, and soap from the roots. Yucca contains saponin which produces a lather when bruised in water. Pioneers, too, used this as soap.

Yucca is the New Mexico state flower.

*DATIL or Indian Banana—like Yucca except that the leaves are 1-1/2″ wide, are bluish-green, channeled, and may be twisted; also, coarse fibers fray out making numerous "curls" along the leaf edges. On dry places, Plains-Foothills, Apr-Aug. Grows from Nevada to Texas, including Mesa Verde and Grand Canyon National Parks. *Yucca baccata.*

SCARLET GILIA (See Red/Stalk)	Trumpet tube flowers 1-2″ long <u>end</u> <u>in 5-point stars</u>; often along one side of stem. <u>Alternate</u> leaves deeply cut.

WHITE/STALK

DARK PENSTEMON (See Blue/Stalk)	Dingy-white tube flowers, <u>end in 2 lips</u>. May hang along one side of stem. <u>Leaves opposite</u>, green, entire.
ARROWHEAD or Duck-Potato	3 petals. Flowers may be whorled (in rows around stem). Leaves—<u>above water</u>—are arrowshaped and 4-16″ long.

If submerged, the leaves are like long ribbons. Found in marshes and shallow water. Fine food for birds and muskrats. Plains-Foothills. *Sagittaria latifolia,* Water-plantain Family.

WHITE LOCO *(p. 76)*	Pea flowers 1/4 to 1″ long, with <u>sharp beak</u> (see Key Terms). <u>Many silvery-hairy leaflets</u>. Plants 4-20″. 2 common species are:

1. **ROCKY MOUNTAIN LOCO**–Flowers are <u>3/4 to 1</u>″ with purple spot on the keel. The 1/2″ calyx is tinged with pink but the sepal tips may be greenish-black.

   Rocky Mountain Loco and the rose-purple Lambert Loco often hybridize, so where the two grow near together one may find colonies of loco varying from white to lavender or pink, with or without the purple spot on the keel.

   The leaves are <u>all basal</u> (very rarely a leaf on the stem) with 11 to 21 leaflets. Plant often grows in large colonies on gravelly slopes and fields, Plains-Subalpine. From Utah and Wyo. south. The pods are either erect or spreading; <u>they never droop</u>. - *Oxytropis sericea,* Pea Family.

2. **DROP-POD LOCO**—The numerous flowers are <u>1/4 to 1/2″ long</u>. The keel may or may not have a purple spot. Leaves are <u>chiefly along the stem</u>, each with 25 to 41 leaflets. Plant is common in dry lodgepole forests, Plains-Subalpine, and is circumpolar. The <u>pods always droop</u>. If pods have not yet formed, the position of the oldest flowers (lowest on the stem) will indicate the future position of the pods. *Oxytropis deflexa.*

BALL-HEAD GILIA (See White/Head)	5 petals. Compact cap 2-4″ long of small star flowers. Most leaves are finely cut. <u>Whole plant is hairy</u> and stem may lean.

DRUMMOND MILKVETCH *(p. 76)*	3/4" whitish pea flowers with <u>blunt keel</u> (see Key Terms). Calyx is usually black-hairy. <u>Leafy, gray-hairy flower stems</u>. Silvery-hairy leaves. Many leaflets. Bushy plant, 1-2' tall. In dry fields. Pods droop.

Flowers are very numerous. They are creamy-white or dirty-white with purple-tipped keels. Pods are 1-2" long. Plant has many stout, but soft stems and is very common in spring, often growing in large clumps. Unlike some of its relatives, it is <u>non-poisonous</u> to stock. Occurs mainly east of the Continental Divide, Plains-Montane. *Astragalus drummondii,* Pea Family.

PARRY MILKVETCH *(p. 76)*	Axillary clusters of 3/4" creamy-white pea flowers. Many leaflets. <u>Soft, gray-hairy, tufted plants 2-5" high</u>. <u>Pods turn upwards</u>.

The side petals often conceal the purplish spot on the keel. Leaves may be taller than the flower stems. Plant grows in sandy, rocky soil, Foothills-Montane. In Wyo. and Colo. *Astragalus parryi,* Pea Family.

NOTE. Plants of this genus were named Milkvetch because they were once supposed to increase the milk yield of goats.

CURLED LOUSEWORT or Parrots-Beak or Sickletop Lousewort or Rams Horn or Mountain Figwort *(p. 77)*	5/8", 2-lipped flower (see Key Terms) with lower lip spreading; upper lip compressed on the sides and strongly arched inward. Narrow, alternate leaves finely toothed, often reddish.

Flowers are white—rarely creamy-white. The tip of the upper lip may turn sideways. Leaves, 1 to 2-1/2" long, are doubly toothed. Several square, reddish stems, 8-20" tall, grow in a clump in dry forests, chiefly subalpine. *Pedicularis racemosa,* Figwort Family.

DEATH CAMAS or Wand-lily *(p. 77)*	6 lobes, <u>each with greenish spot at base</u>. Several creamy-white, 1/2" star flowers. Yellow-tipped stamens. Tufts of <u>grass-like leaves</u>.

The 3 sepals and 3 petals are all alike and at the base of each is a heart-shaped, sticky spot. Plant is 8-18" tall. Foothills-Alpine. A dwarf form occurs in high altitudes. *Zigadenus elegans,* Lily Family.

WHITE/STALK

NOTE. Wand-lily contains alkaloids poisonous to both man and livestock. Another species is even more poisonous and both look very much alike although Zigadenus elegans has larger flowers, less crowded. No zigadenus should be even tasted.

WHITE-FLOWERED PEAVINE *(p. 77)*	A few pea flowers on <u>a vine</u>. Leaves tipped with tendrils or bristles; 4 to 10 leaflets. Stems usually spreading.

The few creamy-white flowers turn light brown as they fade. The end leaflet is replaced by either a bristle or a tendril. Plant is a vine with delicate 6-20″ stems which trail along the ground or may climb—sometimes are nearly erect. It grows on hillsides and banks, often in dense colonies, Plains-Subalpine. From Utah and Wyo. to Ariz. and New Mex. *Lathyrus leucanthus*, Pea Family.

WESTERN VIRGINS BOWER *(p. 77)*	4 or 5 separated "petals." Masses of 1/2″ star flowers on vine. Showy stamens. Opposite leaves with 5 to 7 pinnate leaflets.

Flowers have petal-like sepals (clematis has no true petals). The vine blooms so profusely as to cover whole bushes or rocks with white or creamy masses. The leaflets have petioles and are slightly lobed or toothed. Vine is semi-woody and up to 20 feet in length, climbing over shrubs, trees, and rocks. It is common along roadsides and valleys in the Foothills. In late summer the silky, feathery plumes of the fruits are conspicuous. *Clematis ligusticifolia,* Buttercup Family.

WOODLAND-STAR or Fringe-cup	5 petals, <u>each cut into 3 or more parts</u>. Leaves much divided. Stem often has tiny, red bulblets.

Flowers are sometimes pinkish. Delicate reddish stem. Plant grows in shade in Montane zone; Colo. north. *Lithophragma glabra,* Saxifrage Family.

DOTTED SAXIFRAGE *(p. 77)*	5 dotted, separated, oblong petals. Flower 1/2″ or less. <u>Low mat</u> of tiny, rigid, spine-tipped leaves. Among rocks in dry forests.

Flowers are white with red, orange, or purple spots. Leaves have hair along the edges and are crowded into a dense mat, with a few tiny leaves on the stems. Mat may be 1-3′ square. The flower stems rise 2-6″ with a few flowers. Common in rocky places or under evergreens; Montane-Alpine. The name, saxifrage, means "breaker of rocks." *Saxifraga bronchialis,* Saxifrage Family.

STARRY **SOLOMONPLUME** or Wild Lily-of-the Valley *(p. 77)*	6 lobes. Loose cluster 1-3″ long, of 3/8″ <u>star flowers</u>. <u>Alternate leaves,</u> long, entire, 3/4″ to 3″ wide.* Have parallel veins. Plant is <u>never</u> <u>branched.</u>

Flowers have 3 petals and 3 petal-like sepals, widely separated. 3 to 15 flowers are in a terminal cluster. Leaves, <u>3/4 to 1″ wide,</u> are pointed, light green and <u>may be folded.</u> Veins are parallel to the midrib. Plant is leafy, 6″-2′ tall. This is an early foothills flower and is usually found in moist locations, often in clumps, Foothills-Subalpine. *Smilacina stellata,* Lily Family.

***FALSE SOLOMONS SEAL** or Claspleaf Solomonplume is like the preceding except: Flowers are smaller and more numerous—over 15, and the leaves are <u>1-1/2 to 3″ wide;</u> not folded. *Smilacina racemosa.*

MINERS CANDLE *(p. 77)* *(color plate p. 51)*	1/4″, 5-petaled, saucer flowers along a <u>single</u>* bristly, erect spike with long, <u>narrow leaves projecting</u> <u>between flowers.</u>

The flowers look like white forget-me-nots and they are so thick and flat and so closely attached to the stiff stem that it somewhat resembles a white torch. The leaves on the base of the plant continue along up the spike as smaller, linear, leaflike bracts 1-4″ long, and project out horizontally. The stem is stout, unbranched, 6-24″ tall, and covered with stiff, bristly hairs, prickly to the touch. It grows on open, dry fields and hillsides in Colo. and Wyo., Foothills-Montane. *Cryptantha virgata,* Borage Family.

***BUSHY CRYPTANTHA** or Bushy Torch—is very similar to Miners Candle but there are one to several stout, <u>branched stems;</u> and the flowers may be white or creamy-white. *Cryptantha thyrsiflora* and others.

WHITE **SWEET-CLOVER** (See under Yellow Sweet-Clover in Yellow/Stalk) *(p. 77)*	Small pea flowers in <u>long slender</u> <u>clusters</u> that may be erect or may droop. Fragrant. Leaf has 3 leaflets. <u>Usually bushy plant</u> along roads.

BANEBERRY
(p. 77)

Erect head 2″ long of 3/8″ feathery flowers. Leaves are 3 times divided. Shiny berries. Bushy plant. Damp woods.

Flowers appear feathery because there are 4 to 10 small petals very narrow at base, and 3 to 5 small, petal-like bracts, and also numerous protruding stamens. The large leaves have long stalks, and are divided into leaflets, then into smaller leaflets, then these are toothed or lobed. Plant is 1 to 2-1/2′ tall and is found in damp woods, Montane-Subalpine. It is sometimes called China-berry because the glossy berries may be red or white and when white, look as though made of china. Either red or white, the berries are poisonous. *Actaea rubra,* Buttercup Family.

PENNY-CRESS
or Fanweed
(p. 77)

4 petals. At first, 1″ flat clusters of flowers at ends of branches, then the clusters elongate. Leaves oblong or lance-shaped, upper ones clasp stem. Branched plant 6-24″. 1/2″ pods like pennies.

As with many other members of the mustard family, the flowers start blooming in a fairly flat cluster. As they mature, the clusters elongate so that soon there are pods all along most of the flower branches, but a small cluster will continue to bloom at the ends as long as the plant is in flower. The petioled basal leaves wither early, upper leaves clasp the stem with little ears at base. Plant has several upturned branches, all bearing flowers and pods. The pods have a small notch at top, and are erect or spreading; they do not hang down. Penny-cress is abundant in fields and along roads, Plains-Montane. *Thlaspi arvense,* Mustard Family.

SHEPHERDS PURSE
(p. 78)

4 petals. Clusters of small, flat flowers; stamens not visible. 2 kinds of leaves; lobed leaves in basal rosette; upper leaves clasp stem with ears. Triangular pods.

Upper leaves are lance-shaped and alternate with 2 pointed "ears". The branched stem, 4-18″ tall, grows in fields and waste places; is a common weed in gardens. The pods are notched at top and never hang down. Plains-Foothills. *Capsella bursa pastoris,* Mustard Family.

72

CLASPING PEPPERWEED or Peppergrass *(p. 78)*	4 petals. 1/4″ flowers along many stalks on upper half of main stem. <u>Lower leaves finely divided; upper ones overlap behind stem.</u> Much branched plant 6-24″.

Flowers are very numerous; are white, sometimes tinged with yellow or green. Pods, notched at top, are oval and rounded. The lower leaves are divided into linear parts, the upper ones, small and rounded, clasp the stem, overlapping behind it. Most pepperweeds (there are 8 species) are much branched, with the branch tops at different levels. They often have 2 kinds of leaves. There are many flowers, and the pods are rounded to ovate and do not hang down. Pepperweed is very common along roads and in waste places, Plains-Foothills. *Lepidium perfoliatum,* Mustard Family.

PROBABLY A MUSTARD Many mustards have no common name.	Small clusters of tiny flat flowers with 4 petals, and small alternate leaves.

NOTE TO FLOWER HUNTER! If all these members of the Mustard Family are confusing, don't feel concerned. Remember that the Mustard Family has around 125 species, large and small, in Colorado alone and even the botanists have to get out their lens and books and study both flowers and pods to identify many of them.

Just say to yourself, "H'm—it's a cluster of small white (or yellow) flowers with (A) 4 petals arranged in the form of a cross, (B) the leaves are alternate. So it's some kind of mustard."

Then go merrily on your way.

TWISTED-STALK *(p. 78)*	6 lobes. 1 (or 2) 1/3″ bell flowers on a thread-like stem <u>hide under a broad leaf.</u> Leaves parallel-veined. Branches usually arched. Non-hairy plant near water.

The tiny flower stem at the leaf axil twists abruptly, placing the creamy or greenish-white flower behind or under the leaf. These dainty little bells are not likely to be noticed without a search. Leaves are alternate, pointed, and 2-3″ wide. Plant, 1-3′ high, grows in moist woods and near creeks, Foothills-Subalpine. The stems are branched and arching, hence the flowers and red berries hang from their lower sides. Mont. to New Mex. *Streptopus amplexifolius,* Lily Family.

FAIRYBELLS—Similar to Twisted-stalk but rather rare; has one to several small bell flowers that hang from the tip of the stem and are plainly visible. *Disporum trachycarpum,* Lily Family. *(p. 78)*

BROOK SAXIFRAGE *(p. 78)*	5 petals. 1/4″ star flowers widely scattered over top of plant. Pedicels often reddish. Leaves basal only, shiny, rounded, on long petioles. Slender stem in wet places.

Leaves are coarsely toothed and 1 to 2-1/2″ across. Plant, 10-18″ tall, is common among rocks at the edge of water; Montane-Subalpine. Grows from Mont. to New Mex. *Saxifraga odontoloma, or arguta,* Saxifrage Family.

TALL WHITE **BOG-ORCHID** *(p. 78)*	Small, pure white orchid flowers (see Key Terms). Lip is broad at base, tapering to tip, has tiny spur. Leaves alternate and basal. Erect stem 6-24″ tall. Wet places.

All Habenaria orchids have a small spur attached to the lip of each little flower. Side petals are like wings. Flowers are fragrant and the spur projects outward. Hybridization may produce flowers slightly yellowish or greenish-white. Leaves are pointed, 1/2 to 4″ long, and shiny green. The sturdy stem grows in or beside water, Montane-Subalpine; June-Sep. This is one of the tallest bog-orchids and is found thru-out the region, especially in Glacier National Park. *Habenaria dilatata,* Orchid Family.

LADIES-TRESSES *(p. 78)*	1/4″ orchid flowers spiral upward around the twisted stem. Narrow leaves. In damp, grassy places.

Flowers are pure white and fragrant, with a fiddle-shaped lip. Leaves, narrow lance-shape, are mostly basal with a few alternate. Plant is bright green, fleshy-looking and 4-18″ tall. It grows around lakes and bogs, Foothills-Subalpine, and is easily overlooked among the surrounding grasses and sedges. *Spiranthes romanzoffiana,* Orchid Family.

SNOWBALL **SAXIFRAGE** (See White/Head)	At first, a ball-like cluster of tiny cup flowers. Later this separates into several clusters along a single stem. 5 petals. No stem leaves; basal rosette of smooth leathery leaves.

SCORPION-WEED
(p. 78)

5 petals. Tiny pale cup flowers in clusters curved like a fiddle neck. Stamens protrude. Alternate leaves, some with lobes near base. Plant dusty-green; stiff-hairy.

Flowers, white or bluish, are often numerous, and are coiled in spiral clusters. Sometimes they are coiled only at the tip of the stem. Leaves are lance-shaped and strongly veined on the back. Usually have one or more small, entire lobes near the base of the lower leaves. The stout stem, or stems, are 4-30" tall and are generally erect but may spread around the ground. Plant grows along roadsides and on disturbed soil, Foothills-Montane. *Phacelia heterophylla,* Waterleaf Family.

A similar species of Scorpion-weed, *Phacelia hastata,* has purplish to white flowers and silvery, irregularly lobed leaves.

WATER-CRESS
(p. 78)

4 petals. Clusters of small, inconspicuous flowers. Pinnate, glossy leaflets with largest one at the end. Forms mats in water or wet places.

Flowers are in crowded clusters, both terminal and axillary. Plant is trailing in running water or muddy places. The stems root at the nodes, roots that are white and thread-like. Water-cress is common along stream banks, Plains-Foothills. *Rorippa nasturtium-aquaticum,* Mustard Family.

NOTE. The peppery shoots are served in salads but should be used only if grown in uncontaminated water. It has been eaten since the days of the ancient Persians and the Romans.

SPEARMINT
(p. 78)

Tiny, irregular, 5-petaled flowers in small clusters at ends of square stems. Opposite, toothed leaves. Spearmint fragrance.

Flowers are white (sometimes pinkish) and are obscurely 2-lipped. Leaves are lance-shaped or ovate, and sessile or nearly so. Stems are 4-12" high. Plant prefers damp soil but is widespread, Plains-Montane. *Mentha spicata,* Mint Family.

NOTES. Spearmint is obtained from this species and its leaves, steeped in hot water, make delicious tea.

Other useful members of the Mint Family include hoarhound, marjoram, oregano, peppermint, sage, thyme, and lavender. The seasoning agent, sage, comes from the Mint Family and not from

WHITE/STALK

sagebrush as the name might suggest. Sagebrush is a shrub with a bitter juice and an odor like that of the true sage.

NORTHERN BEDSTRAW *(p. 78)*	4 petals. Masses of tiny saucer flowers, both terminal and axillary. Small <u>leaves in rows of 4</u>. Square stem 6-28″.

Flowers are fragrant and white or creamy. Leaves, 1/2 to 2″ long, are whorled, i.e., 4 leaves circle the stem at each node or joint. Plant is abundant on both dry, sunny slopes and moist, shady places. Foothills-Subalpine. *Galium boreale,* Madder Family.

NOTES. At one time, the fragrant dried foliage was used as a substitute for straw in mattress ticking.
   A purple dye can be made from the roots of most bedstraws. Coffee, quinine, ipecac and gardenias also belong to the Madder Family.

ALPINE BISTORT *(p. 78)*	<u>Very slim spike</u> of tiny flowers above tiny brownish bulblets along grass-like stem 3-10″ high. Leaves alternate and basal; linear.

White or pinkish flowers, have protruding stamens. Basal leaves are 1/2 to 4″ long; stem leaves are smaller. The single stem is inconspicuous, growing on tundra and high meadows, Subalpine-Alpine. *Polygonum viviparum,* Buckwheat Family.

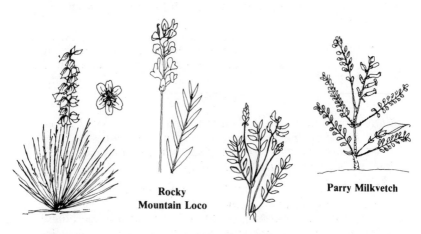

Yucca

Rocky Mountain Loco

Drummond Milkvetch

Parry Milkvetch

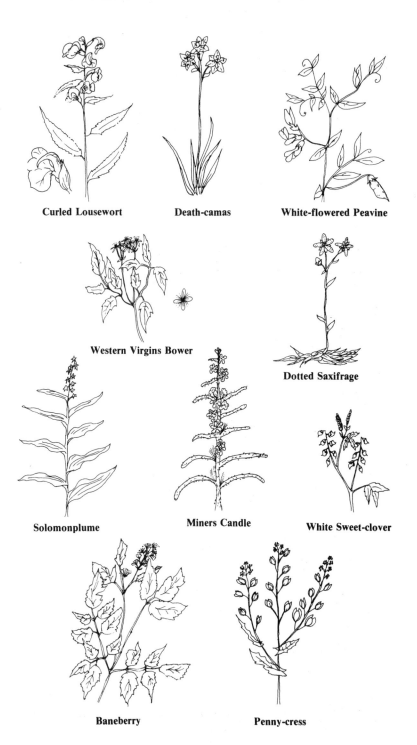

Curled Lousewort

Death-camas

White-flowered Peavine

Western Virgins Bower

Dotted Saxifrage

Solomonplume

Miners Candle

White Sweet-clover

Baneberry

Penny-cress

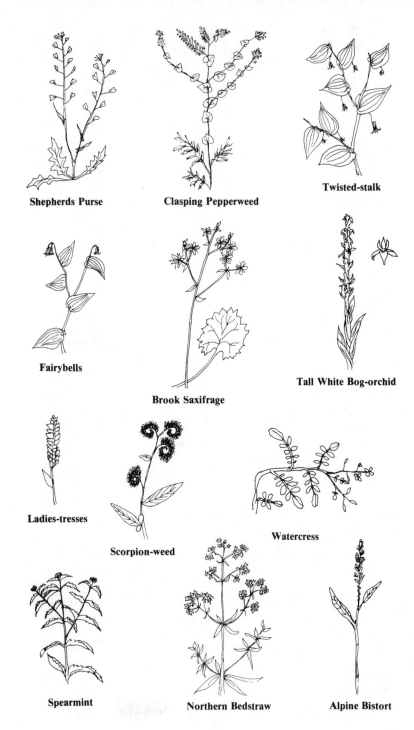

Shepherds Purse

Clasping Pepperweed

Twisted-stalk

Fairybells

Brook Saxifrage

Tall White Bog-orchid

Ladies-tresses

Scorpion-weed

Watercress

Spearmint

Northern Bedstraw

Alpine Bistort

78

NORTHERN BEARGRASS	6 lobes. Many small flowers in a large cone-shaped head. Leaves grass-like and dense. Stout, coarse plant 3-6' tall.

Numerous creamy-white flowers in a compact head several inches long. Thick tufts of grass-like, tough, sharp-edged leaves; stem leaves are smaller. Plant often grows in colonies but does not bloom every year, so some seasons there may be many big, striking, showy heads, and other years almost none. In Mont. and Idaho. *Zerophyllum tenax,* Lily Family.

COW PARSNIP or Hercules Parsnip or Bears Breeches *(p. 87)* *(color plate p. 51)*	5 petals. 2-10" compound umbels of 3/8" flat flowers; those around the outside of the cluster are larger. Huge leaf bases sheathe stem. Leaves palmately divided. Near creeks. 2-8' tall.

Occasionally the petals are deeply and irregularly lobed. Buds are green. Leaves are commonly divided into 3 great leaflets, always from the tip of the petiole. Each leaflet is 4-12" broad, 4-16" long, and is coarsely toothed, or lobed and toothed.

Sometimes the Cow Parsnip leaves are not divided completely into 3 separate leaflets but are merely divided partway into 3 big, palmate, toothed lobes at the tip of the stem.

The leaf stalks have wide bases which sheathe (wrap around) the stems conspicuously and for this reason the plant is sometimes called "Bears Breeches." The stem is tall, stout, thick, and very silky-hairy. Plant grows in swampy places along or near streams. Foothills-Subalpine. *Heracleum lanatum,* Carrot Family.

NOTES. Cow Parsnip was named Heracleum for Hercules, because of its great size.

It is eaten by big game and domestic animals. Indians use it for food. If carefully peeled, the juicy young stems are edible but no member of the carrot family should be even tasted because some very similar-looking species are deadly poisonous.

The Carrot Family is very large. Only a few of the most common and easily recognized species are described in this book. The flowers are in umbels and are almost always yellow or white. (Of course, not all flowers that bloom in umbels belong to this family.) Anise, caraway, carrots, celery, coriander, dill, parsley and parsnips are all members of the Carrot Family.

WHITE/HEAD

POISON HEMLOCK
(p. 88)

> 5 petals. 2-8″ compound umbels of dainty, tiny flowers. Large, delicate fern leaves. Purple spots on stems. Plant is 3-8′ tall.

The delicate flowers are white or off-white. Leaves, 4-10″ wide, are as finely dissected as lace. Their petioles clasp the stem. Plant has tall, hollow, branched stems spotted with purple. It prefers moist soil and irrigated places around towns, and grows over much of the world. Plains-Montane. *Conium maculatum,* Carrot Family.

NOTE. This is the poison hemlock which Socrates was forced to drink.

WATER HEMLOCK
(p. 88)

> 5 petals. 2-4″ compound umbels of tiny flowers. Lance-shaped leaflets. Leaf veins end in notches. Stem 2-5′. Wet places.

The large leaves, whose petioles sheathe the stem, are divided into leaflets that are then divided into smaller leaflets that are toothed and are 1-4″ long. The best identification of the Water Hemlock lies in the leaf veins which end in the notches between the teeth instead of at or toward the tips of the teeth as is the case with most plants. Plant has stout stems and grows along streams, often standing in water. Plains-Foothills. *Cicuta douglasii,* Carrot Family

NOTE. This and the Poison Hemlock are our most poisonous plants.

GIANT ANGELICA
(p. 88)

> 2-3″ globe-shaped umbels of tiny flowers. Leaves usually twice divided; ovate leaflets. Leaf bases sheathe plant stem. Purple-shaded stems, 3-6′. Wet places.

Flowers are in compound or double umbels. Both the large and the small umbels are ball-shaped. There are 30 to 45 little stems or "spokes" in the big umbel. After the white petals drop, the umbels, with their developing fruits, look greenish or brown. The large leaves are divided into leaflets that are themselves divided into smaller, ovate, toothed leaflets. The coarse, stout stems are generally purple-shaded but are not dotted. Angelica grows in wet meadows and along streams. Foothills-Montane. Chiefly in Wyo. and Colo. *Angelica ampla,* Carrot Family.

A species of lovage—**PORTER LOVAGE**—looks much like Giant

Angelica but the flower umbels are flat, with 11 to 24 tiny stems in the umbel; the leaves are more finely divided—fernlike; and the plant, 1-1/2 to 3' tall, is branched and is never purplish. It is very common in valleys, woods, and on slopes; from Wyoming south and west. *Ligusticum porteri,* Carrot Family. *(p. 88)*

| **WHITETOP** Or Whiteweed *(p. 88)* | 4 petals. Masses of 1/4" flowers form a wide, flat cluster at top of branched plant 8-20" tall; often in dense stands. Alternate leaves. Tiny pods usually heart-shaped. |

The branches rise from different points along the main stem but together they support a wide, compact, flat-topped cluster of flowers. Flowers are white or creamy with yellow to greenish stamens. Leaves are ovate to oblong and clasp the stem. Because it spreads from a horizontal root system, White-top blooms in filmy masses along roadsides and in fields, visible from some distance. Apr.-Jul. Plains-Foothills. Although attractive, this weed is very difficult to eradicate. Pods are erect or spreading. *Cardaria draba,* Mustard Family.

| **COMMON BALL-HEAD GILIA** *(p. 88)* | 5 petals. Cluster 2-4" long of 1/4" white star flowers. Leaves linear or linear-divided. Whole plant is cobwebby-hairy and stem may lean. 1 foot tall or less. |

Flowers form a cap that may be round or cone-shaped. They are thickly set with bracts shorter than the flowers. The stem often leans as though bent by the weight of the flower head. Leaves are alternate and linear or cut into linear divisions. Found on dry plains and foothills from So. Dak. to Ore. and south to Nebr., Utah and Calif. *Ipomopsis, or Gilia congesta,* Phlox Family.

ALPINE BALL-HEAD GILIA—is very similar but the flowers are creamy-white and fragrant; the flower head is round; and the plant is strictly alpine. *Ipomopsis globularis.*

| **ELK THISTLE** or Drummond Thistle or Everts Thistle *(p. 89)* | Cluster of 1 to 8 brushy heads, 1-2" wide of disk flowers only. Usually dingy-white. Bracts spiny and twisted. Very prickly plant 4-36". Occurs in 2 forms. |

Flowers may be creamy to pink or pale purple but are often dingy-white. The bracts have hair only along their edges. The outer bracts

81

end in spines; inner bracts are twisted and often "chewed."

Elk Thistle is common in damp mountain meadows and along stream banks. Montane-Subalpine. Elk and bears are fond of this plant. It occurs in 2 forms: tall and short; but both have the same botanical name. *Cirsium coloradense, or drummondii,* Composite Family.

1. **ELK THISTLE**—tall form. Heads are sessile in a dense cluster at the top of stem. There may also be heads in the upper leaf axils. Leaves are alternate, narrow, and prickly; green above and paler below. Small leaves often extend above the top flower cluster. The stout, unbranched stem, 1-1/2 to 3' high is almost as thick at the top as at the bottom. It may be green to reddish-brown.
2. **ELK THISTLE**—short form. Flowers bloom in a cluster at ground level in the center of a dense leaf rosette. This form has no plant stem, just the very attractive leaf rosette less than 8" high and 1 to 2-1/2' across, in the center of which—when the plant is blooming—lies a cluster of stemless flowers and buds. Leaves, 6" wide or more, and up to 14" long, are light green on top and silvery below with either a white or a purplish midrib, and are very prickly.

NOTE. Elk Thistle saved Truman Everts from starvation in Yellowstone Park in 1870. A member of the first thorough exploration party in the Park, he became separated from his companions, was thrown from his horse, and his spectacles were broken. Lost, without a horse, and extremely near-sighted, he still managed to survive, principally upon this plant, until he was rescued over a month later.

For other dingy-white to gray thistles look in Other Colors/Head.

ARCTIC GENTIAN (See Other Colors/Head)	Cluster of cup-shaped flowers about 1-1/4" deep; dotted inside and streaked outside with purple. Salmon-pink stamens. Narrow leaves. Plant 3-8" tall.
BROOK-CRESS or Bitter-Cress *(p. 89)* *(color plate p. 51)*	4 petals. 2" head (cluster) of 1/2" bright saucer flowers. Leaves alternate, heart-shaped, coarsely toothed. Near water.

Flowers are a lovely, clear white. Petals have a faint tinge of green at the base. Leaves are bright green, pointed, and 1-2" long. Plant grows abundantly along streams, with erect, leafy stems 10-30" tall. Needle-like pods; erect or nearly so. *Cardamine cordifolia,* Mustard Family.

STICKY CINQUEFOIL	5 petals. Cluster of saucer flowers.
or Creamy Cinquefoil	Usually 5 to 9 leaflets sharply
(p. 89)	toothed. Stout, erect, sticky-hairy plant.

The white or creamy petals are slightly longer than the sepals. The hairy, pinnate leaflets often decrease irregularly in size from tip to base of leaf. The stems, 1-3' tall, are hairy and may be reddish-tinged. Grows in meadows. Foothills-Subalpine. *Potentilla arguta,* Rose Family.

YARROW	1 to 2-1/2" flat cluster of 1/4"
(p. 89)	flowers with 4 to 6 tiny, oblong,
(color plate p. 52)	petal-like rays. Bracts have dark edges. Very narrow, fern-like, gray-green leaves.

The compact clusters are nearly always white but may rarely be pale pink or lavender. The buds are dark gray. Leaves are finely dissected into rather crowded divisions, and are aromatic. Plant is erect and 4" to 2-1/2" feet tall. It is very common, June-Sep. in all zones. *Achillea lanulosa and A. millefolium,* Composite Family.

NOTES. Yarrow is actually a composite ("Daisy" type) with small, oblong rays and a tiny center of whitish to pale yellow disk flowers. It has been placed here in Heads because it looks like a flat-topped head of small flowers with little, white petals.

Yarrow is probably closely related to a plant used by Achilles to treat the wounds of his soldiers. We use it as a tonic, as did the Indians. If cows eat Yarrow their milk has a disagreeable taste.

The species name, millefolium, means "thousand leaves"; lanulosa means "woolly".

AMERICAN BISTORT	Dense heads 1" wide and 1 to 2-1/2"
(p. 89)	long, of tiny cup flowers. Projecting stamens. Stem leaves few, small, and sheathe stems. Basal leaves long, narrow, entire.

Projecting stamens give the heads a somewhat fuzzy appearance, and from a distance, the stems look as though topped with a puff of white cotton—or sometimes pink cotton, because as they age the flower heads may turn pink. When going to seed, the heads appear to be covered with small, brown scales. Plant, 4-24" tall, sways

WHITE/HEAD

83

easily in the wind, and is very common in damp ground. Subalpine—Alpine. The stems may be either red or green. *Polygonum bistortoides,* Buckwheat Family.

NOTE. The Buckwheat Family includes two well-known food plants: the cereal grain, common buckwheat; and the garden fruit, rhubarb. Nearly everyone has eaten rhubarb stems but not everybody is aware that the leaves themselves are poisonous because they contain oxalic acid.

FERN-LEAF CANDYTUFT	4 petals. Cluster of 1/2″ flowers. Leaves alternate, much divided. Stem leaves do not clasp. Unbranched plant 2-8″. 1/3″ pods taper at both ends. Alpine only.

Flowers are white or pink—and fragrant. Hairy leaves are pinnately divided into narrow parts. There are always old leaf bases on root crown. Plant is tufted. Colo. and Utah north. *Smelowskia calycina,* Mustard Family.

COWBANE (p. 89)	5 petals. 1 to 2-1/2″ umbels of small white flowers. No bracts at base of umbel. Leaves once divided; usually 7 ovate leaflets. Stem 1-1/2 to 3′. Wet places.

The 7 to 9 toothed leaflets are about 1″ long. There are only a few leaves and their bases sheathe the stem. From Wyo. and Utah to New Mex., Montane-Subalpine. *Oxypolis fendleri,* Carrot Family.

YAMPA	5 petals. Loose umbels of tiny white flowers. Leaves have narrow, grasslike leaflets 1-6″ long, which wither early. Erect, slender stem 1-3′.

Umbels are compound as in most of the carrot family. Stem is non-hairy and usually solitary. Valleys and meadows. Foothills-Montane. *Perideridia gairdneri,* Carrot Family.

NOTES. This was a favorite food of the Indians, also of early explorers and pioneers. Beware, however, of confusing it with similar, poisonous species.

Yampa is scattered over the Rockies; abundant in some areas but absent from many others. It was common in the Yampa River valley in N.W. Colorado and the river, the valley and the town of Yampa were all named for it. Among names considered for the new state of Colorado, Yampa ranked high.

PEARLY EVERLASTING
(p. 90)
(color plate p. 51)

Heads of little flowers like tiny snowballs; no rays or petals. Leaves narrow, and white on lower side. Plant 1-2' tall. Often in masses.

The tiny disk flowers may have a greenish-yellow tint, but usually the small round heads look pearly white because each little flower is wrapped in papery, white bracts. Flowers turn brown with age. Leaves are alternate, sessile, entire, 1-4" long, gray-green above and cottony white below. The basal leaves wither early. Plant is coated with cobwebby hairs and may be greenish to silvery. It is frequently seen in masses along roads and on rocky slopes from the foothills up but especially in the subalpine zone. *Anaphalis margaritacea,* Composite Family.

NOTE. Pearly Everlasting might be confused with Tall Pussytoes but:

Pearly Everlasting	Tall Pussytoes
Often grows in clumps.	Usually occurs singly.
Leaves green or gray above; silvery below.	Leaves always silvery both sides.
Plant 10-24" tall	Plant 6-16" tall.
Lower leaves are 1-4" long.	Basal leaves are 4-6" long.

WILD CANDYTUFT
or Mountain Candytuft
(p. 90)

4 petals. Cluster of 3/8" flat flowers at top of unbranched 1-10" stem. Stamens not visible. Basal leaves are in rosette; upper ones clasp stem with little ears. Pods heart-shaped.

Flowers may start blooming when plant is only 1" or 2" high. They open first around the outer edge of a flat head of brownish-purplish buds. Flowers are rarely purple-tinged. Leaves are grayish to dark green, and oval or spoon-shaped. The stem or stems are quite leafy and may grow in small clumps. Candytuft is one of the earliest flowers in the foothills, blooming later, of course, in higher altitudes. Apr.-Jul. It prefers moist places. Foothills-Alpine. Pods are erect or spreading; do not hang down. *Thlaspi alpestre,* Mustard Family.

WHITE/HEAD

SNOWBALL SAXIFRAGE
(p. 90)

> 5 petals. At first, a <u>ball-like cluster</u> of tiny cup flowers. Later this separates into several clusters along a single stem. <u>No stem leaves</u>; basal rosette of <u>smooth leathery leaves</u>.

Flowers are white but each one is nestled in small bracts that are sometimes dark-colored and this may give a greenish-yellow cast to the flowers. Leaves are ovate or oblong, short-petioled, and may be toothed. They may lie flat at the base of the plant, or turn upwards, or turn down like an inverted bowl. The single stem, 2-12″ tall, grows on open ground from Mont. to New Mex. and starts blooming in early spring. Apr.-Aug. Foothills-Alpine. *Saxifraga rhomboidea,* Saxifrage Family.

PUSSYTOES
(p. 90)

> 1/2 to 1″ clusters of flowers like tiny snowballs. <u>No rays or petals.</u> Entire, silvery leaves 1/2 to 6″ long. <u>Whole plant silvery</u> and 1-16″ tall. 2 species follow.

1. **MOUNTAIN PUSSYTOES**—Heads are of tiny, white disk flowers only—sometimes pinkish. Leaves, 1/2 to 1″ long, have rounded tips but no petioles. Plant <u>forms silvery mats</u> from which the white <u>flower stems rise 1-6″.</u> Abundant in dry, sunny meadows. Foothills-Subalpine. *Antennaria parvifolia,* Composite Family.

2. **TALL PUSSYTOES**—The disk flowers are always white. Stem leaves are small; <u>basal leaves are 4-6″</u> long and are strongly 3-nerved. This pussytoe <u>does not form mats. Its silvery stems are 6-16″ long</u> and are strongly 3-nerved. This pussytoe does not form mats. Its silvery stems are 6-16″ tall and it occurs scatteringly in rather shady places and moist forests. Colo. to Mont. *Antennaria anaphaloides or pulcherrima.*

SAND ONION
(p. 90)

> 6 petals and sepals; 1″ umbel of 1/8″ flowers. Tips of inner petals spread out. <u>Usually 2 grass-like, grooved leaves</u>.

The tiny white flowers (rarely pink) are in an erect umbel on a leafless stem. Leaves are channeled or grooved. When crushed, they have a strong onion smell. Plant has a slender stem 1′ or less, and it grows in rather dry places. Apr.-Sep. Plains-Montane. Sometimes it intergrades with the usually pink Wild Onion. *Allium textile,* Lily Family.

WHITE DUTCH CLOVER *(p. 90)*	Round clusters of tiny pea flowers (see Key Terms). <u>Tiny reddish spots between teeth of calyx.</u> Leaf has 3 leaflets. <u>Creeping</u>, leafy plant.

Compact flower heads on long stems. The leaflets often have a white spot. This clover, with numerous flower heads and creeping, often rooting stems, is common along roadsides and in meadows. Apr.-Oct. Plains-Subalpine. *Trifolium repens,* Pea Family.

INDIAN HEMP (See under Spreading Dogbane in Red/Head)	5 petals. Small clusters of tiny whitish flowers, urn-shaped. Leaves opposite, entire, usually ascending.

ROCK-JASMINE or Rock-Primrose *(p. 90)*	5 petals. <u>Loose spreading umbel of 1/8″ flowers.</u> Reddish sepals. Wee leaves in <u>basal rosette only</u>. <u>Thread-like stem.</u> Plant 1-7″.

The star-like flowers are in double umbels with small bracts at base of main umbel. Petals are shorter than the usually reddish-brown sepals. The tiny leaves may be either green or red. The single, erect stem is like a delicate green or reddish wire. Although it is very common and widely distributed, Foothills-Alpine, the little plant is easily overlooked. *Androsace septentrionalis,* Primrose Family.

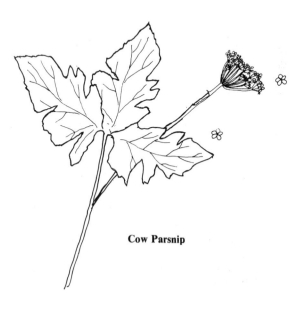

Cow Parsnip

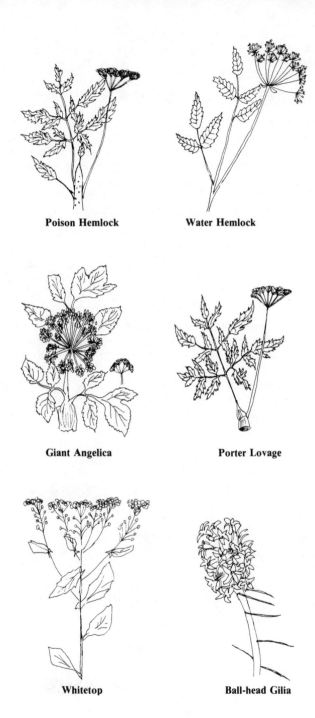

Poison Hemlock

Water Hemlock

Giant Angelica

Porter Lovage

Whitetop

Ball-head Gilia

Elk Thistle

Brookcress

Sticky Cinquefoil

Yarrow

American Bistort

Cowbane

Pearly Everlasting

Wild Candytuft

Snowball Saxifrage

Mountain Pussytoes

Rock-jasmine

Sand Onion

White Dutch Clover

90

WHITE EVENING-STAR or Blazing Star or Stickleaf *(p. 99)*	Usually 10 petals. 2-4″ (or 6″*) star flowers, creamy-white to pale yellow. Many long stamens. A few rough, alternate, "clingy" leaves. Open in late afternoon.

Petals surround a center of 30 or more stamens. The flowers open in late afternoon, so anyone passing a bed of them during the day would see only thin, weedy-looking growth, but at dusk he would find a mass of lovely, creamy-white, starry blossoms which open so rapidly that the movement of the petals can be observed. Leaves are coarsely toothed—sometimes lobed—and are covered with stiff, barbed hair that sticks tightly to clothing. White, rather shiny branches spread out from a rough, woody stem 12-20″ tall. Plant prefers sandy soil; Plains-Foothills. *Mentzelia nuda,* Loasa Family.

*GIANT EVENING STAR—is very similar to the preceding but is a larger plant—1-3′, and the flowers are usually 4-6″ wide, and are fragrant. It is seldom seen because it grows only on a certain kind of shale soil, and the flowers open after sunset. *Mentzelia decapetala.*

PRICKLY POPPY *(p. 99)* *(color plate p. 54)*	3″ flower, usually 6 big paper-like petals. Many 1/2″ yellow stamens around one dark pistil. Tall prickly plant.

Leaves are large, lobed and gray-green with sharp, yellow spines. Prickly Poppy is a silvery, thistle-like plant, 2-5′ tall, with yellow milky juice. It is very common along roadways and stony slopes, Plains-Foothills; May-Sep.; from Wyo. to New Mex. *Argemone polyanthemos,* or *intermedia,* Poppy Family.

WHITE STEMLESS EVENING-PRIMROSE *(p. 100)*	4 wide petals, rounded. 3″ flower. Long stamens have rod-like tips. Leaves basal. Near ground level—no plant stem.

The showy, fragrant flower opens in late afternoon and withers under the next day's sun, turning pink with age. The 4 sepals, too, are pinkish and their tips turn down loosely. Leaves,3-6″ long, are thin and toothed or lobed. Plant is like a rosette and grows on sunny, dry, rocky slopes; Plains-Montane. From Colo. south. *Oenothera caespitosa,* Evening-Primrose Family.

NOTE. Around 1900, a Dutch botanist, Hugh De Vries, imported and planted several species of evening-primrose in his garden. In experimenting with them, he obtained new types upon which he based his work on the theory of evolution by mutation.

NUTTALL EVENING-PRIMROSE *(p. 100)*	4 wide petals. 2″ white flower that turns pink with age. Long stamens with <u>rod-like tips.</u> <u>Long, narrow,</u> <u>alternate leaves.</u> <u>Shiny white stems</u> 6-30″.

Flowers are axillary and the pods develop in the leaf axils. Leaves are usually entire. Plant is leafy and woody with a non-hairy, white stem from which layers of bark peel off in shreds. Because it grows from a spreading underground root, it is often found in patches. Foothills-Montane. Colo. north. *Oenothera nuttallii,* Evening-Primrose Family.

WESTERN TRILLIUM or Wakerobin	3 petals. A 1-3″ flower at top of stem. <u>3 leaves, entire, broad,</u> in a circle below the flower. Moist woods.

Petals turn from white to pink to purple. The 3 leaves are ovate. Plant is 8-16″ tall. Montane-Subalpine. From Colo. north. *Trillium ovatum,* Lily Family.

MARIPOSA or Mariposa-lily *(p. 100)* *(color plate p. 54)*	3 wide petals. Erect, tulip-like flower 1 to 1-1/2″ deep. Yellow fringe inside. <u>Few grass-like leaves.</u> 8-20″ tall. 2 common species follow.

The several species of this beautiful lily are generally white but may very from pale pink or lilac to deep pink or purple, even yellow. The outside of the cup is shaded green and there are 3 narrow, greenish sepals. On the inner base of each petal is a gland and beside it, a fringe of hairs. 6 ivory-colored stamens surround a 3-pronged pistil.

1. **MARIPOSA or Gunnisons Mariposa**—The <u>stamens are pointed</u>; the <u>gland</u> on each petal is <u>oblong</u>; the <u>beard</u> near the gland is <u>dense</u>; and the flower is common on the <u>eastern side</u> of the Continental Divide from the foothills to 11,000 feet. *Calochortus gunnisonii,* Lily Family.
2. **SEGO-LILY or Nuttalls Mariposa**—The <u>stamen tips are blunt</u>; the <u>gland</u> at base of petals is <u>circular or crescent-shaped</u>; the <u>beard</u> near the gland is <u>sparse</u>; and the flower is common on the <u>western side</u> of the Continental Divide from Utah and Colo. south. Plains-Montane. *Calochortus nuttallii.*

NOTES. Sego-lily is the Utah state flower. In early days, it was an important source of food for Mormon pioneers, and for Indians. "Mariposa" is the Spanish word for "butterfly."

WHITE GERANIUM or Richardson Geranium *(p. 100)*	5 petals with pink to purple veins. 1 to 1-1/2" flowers. Pointed green sepals. Thin divided leaves with petioles. Single or few plant stems. Flower stems are in pairs.* Prefers shade.

The rounded petals are white to lavender with darker veins. 5 small sepals can often be seen between the petals. Although the flower stems are usually in pairs, *both flowers seldom bloom at the same time. Leaves on long petioles, are circular in outline, and are deeply divided into narrow lobes. The usually single plant stem is 1 to 2-1/2' tall and grows in moist meadows and aspen groves; Foothills-Subalpine. *Geranium richardsonii,* Geranium Family.

ANEMONES *(p. 100)* *(color plate p. 53)*	4 to 7 "petals" not veined. One or more 1-1/4" flowers rise from a leafy collar circling the plant stem. No green sepals. Leaves deeply divided. 3 species follow.

Flowers usually have 5 pure white to yellow sepals that look just like petals (anemones have no true petals.) In the center are numerous stamens and a little greenish cluster of pistils. Below the flower—from 1" to 5" below—is a circle or collar of bracts that are much divided and toothed and look just like the leaves except that they are usually smaller and are sessile. These bracts were at first wrapped around the buds but were left below as the flowers gradually developed and pushed upward. The deeply cut leaves have petioles.

1. **MEADOW ANEMONE**—Flower is pure white and is usually solitary on a long stalk. If not, the central or end flower blooms first. The style (part of the pistil) is straight. Leaves have broad but sharply toothed divisions; basal leaves are generally 4-5" wide. The stem, 8-24" tall, is sometimes branched or forked, usually with a leafy collar and one long-stalked flower on each fork. On ditch banks and meadows, usually below 9,000 feet. *Anemone canadensis,* Buttercup Family.

2. **NARCISSUS ANEMONE or ALPINE ANEMONE**—Flower is lemon yellow to whitish. It may be single but more often there are 2 to 4, all rising from the same collar of bracts and all blooming at about the same time. The styles are short and

curved. The leaf divisions are rather broad, and basal leaves are 2-3″ wide. The stout, hairy stem, 4-16″ tall, grows on meadows, generally above 9,000 feet, up to the tundra. From Colo. north to Alaska and also in the Alps. *Anemone narcissiflora* or *zephyra.*

3. **NORTHERN ANEMONE**—Flower is always single, and is white, sometimes tinged with purple. Leaves have 3 wedge-shaped divisions that may be lobed. Basal leaves are not over 2″ wide. The plant is 4-8″ tall, and is rather dainty. Not common. Found in high, moist woods and above timberline to 13,000 feet. From Colo. north. *Anemone parviflora.*

WHITE MARSH-MARIGOLD *(p. 100)* *(color plate p. 52)*	5 to 15 rounded "petals." 1-1/2″ flowers. Many crowded, yellow stamens. Bluish buds. Leaves basal, ovate to round and 3-8″ wide. In wet places.

The sepals look exactly like petals (there are no true petals). They are pure white when fully open but the outside turns blue or greenish as they age. Leaves are thick, glossy, and dark green; usually have scalloped edges. Plant is 3-10″ high and grows abundantly in bogs or lake margins, especially in the subalpine zone—may even push up through the edge of melting snowbanks. *Caltha leptosepala,* Buttercup Family.

SAND-LILY *(p. 100)*	6 widely separated points. 1-1/4″ pure white star flowers; long white tube. Yellow stamens. Grass-like leaves. Low—no plant stem.

These beautiful, waxy-white lilies have 6 petals and sepals all alike and united in a 1″ flower tube. This is one of the earliest spring flowers—Apr.-Jun. Leaves resemble heavy, curved blades of grass 6″ long. All flowers and leaves rise directly from the root crown. Plant grows in clumps in sandy soil; Plains-Foothills; and after the blooming period ends, it disappears entirely. *Leucocrinum montanum,* Lily Family.

FIELD BINDWEED or Wild Morning-Glory *(p. 100)*	5 petals are joined in a 1″ trumpet flower, pink-striped on back. Alternate leaves have 2 lobes at base. Trailing plant.

Flowers, usually white but sometimes pink, are axillary. The 2 leaf lobes point outward and downward. Plant trails along the ground or twines around other plants and rocks. It is the bane of farmers because it is so persistent and so difficult to eradicate, rapidly taking over whole fields. Despite its undesirable character, its flowers are dainty and often form a delicate white net along roadsides and in cultivated fields. *Convolvulus arvensis,* Morning Glory Family. NOTE. Bindweed belongs to the same family as the cultivated morning glory and the sweet potato. One bush-like morning glory species has a root far bigger than that of the sweet potato but not so palatable.

CUT-LEAF EVENING-PRIMROSE *(p. 101)*	4 petals. Flower, 1/2 to 1-1/4″, turns pink with age. Long, yellow stamens. Sepals turn down. Stem leaves much cut. Low, branched plant, 2-10″.

Flowers are axillary. A 4-lobed pistil is surrounded by 8 stamens. Leaves are narrow and deeply, pinnately cut; may turn red when aging. Basal leaves wither early. Plant is common along roadsides and in waste places. Plains-Montane. *Oenothera coronopifolia,* Evening-Primrose Family.

PRAIRIE EVENING-PRIMROSE—is like the above only—the flower is 1-1/2 to 3″ wide; basal leaves are sometimes entire, the plant is up to 18″ tall, and it blooms chiefly on the plains in sandy soil. *Oenothera albicaulis.*

MOUNTAIN DRYAD or Mountain Avens *(p. 101)*	8 (to 10) petals. 1″ flower. Leaves small, alternate, scalloped, white below; and their edges turn under. Plant forms mats on tundra. Alpine.

Flowers usually have 8 white or creamy-white petals, and numerous stamens. Calyx may be black-hairy. Leaves, 1/4 to 1″ long, have conspicuous veins. This is the largest white-flowered, mat-forming plant in the alpine zone and is actually a creeping shrub. Grows on gravel slopes from Colo. to Alaska, also in Greenland. *Dryas octopetala,* Rose Family. NOTES. Octopetala means 8 petals. Mtn. Dryad is an important source of food for the ptarmigan, a large, grouse-like bird that lives on the tundra.

WOOD-NYMPH or Single-Delight *(p. 101)* *(color plate p. 53)*	4 or 5 wide petals. A single 1″ star flower <u>faces down</u>. Petals are <u>ruffled</u>. No pink. Prominent pistil. Leaves round; all basal. Plant <u>under 4″</u>. <u>Shady forests</u>.

The stamen tips lying against the white or creamy-white petals look like tiny yellow or greenish spots. Flower is fragrant. Leaves are

WHITE/SAUCER

shiny, finely toothed and evergreen. Plant is fleshy and grows in moist, subalpine, evergreen forests; is circumpolar. The flower is delicate and beautiful, worth getting down on the ground to see. It is becoming rare. *Pyrola,* or *Moneses uniflora,* Heath Family.

FRINGED PARNASSIA or Fringed Grass-of-Parnassus	5 fringed petals. A single 3/4" star flower at top of stem. A <u>single leaf</u> <u>clasps middle of stem</u>; other leaves basal.

Basal leaves entire and heart-shaped, with petioles. Wet places, Montane-Alpine. Colo. north. *Parnassia fimbriata,* Saxifrage Family.

GRASS-OF-PARNASSUS—or Small-flowered Parnassia—like the above except that the petals are not fringed; the leaves are ovate; and the single stem leaf is usually below the middle. Foothills-Subalpine. *Parnassia parviflora..*

MOUNTAIN PHLOX or Rock Hill Phlox *(p. 101)* *(color plate p. 52)*	3/4" flat flowers with 5 petals. Stamens are inside the slender tube. Short needle-like leaves form a <u>loose</u> <u>mat</u> 1-4" high.

The numerous flowers may be white, pink, pale blue, or lavender. A single flower tops each little stem. Petals are rounded; may be notched. Note the very small opening of the flower tube from which the petals spread out—a characteristic of phlox. This widespread species is our most common phlox. Foothills-Montane. *Phlox multiflora,* Phlox Family.

ALPINE PHLOX—has flowers like the above but they are either white or pale blue. The tiny leaves are crowded into a <u>dense, little</u> <u>cushion</u> about 1-1/2" high, sometimes entirely covered with flowers. <u>Subalpine-Alpine</u>. *Phlox pulvinata—or caespitosa.*

NOTE. All varieties of phlox cultivated in flower gardens today have been developed from wild species.

WILD STRAWBERRY *(p. 101)*	5 rounded petals. Showy stamens. Leaves have <u>3 leaflets,</u> coarsely toothed and veined. <u>Low plant</u>.

Flowers have many stamens and pistils. 3 leaflets spread out from the end of a long petiole, and are toothed mainly around their tips. The 2-4" plant sends out runners that root at the tips, thus producing new plants. It grows in meadows and woods, Foothills-Subalpine. *Fragaria ovalis,* Rose Family.

NOTES. Unlike most plants, strawberries have their seeds on the surface of the fruit.

Indians ate the berries and made tea from the leaves. The berries are eaten by birds, bears, turtles, rodents and other wild life.

CANADA VIOLET *(color plate p. 52)*	5 petals. 3/4″ slightly irregular flower has crook in stem neck. The lower petal is veined and <u>becomes a spur in back</u>.

Flowers are white with lavender veins and are usually shaded on the back with purple. Flowers are axillary. Leaves are heart-shaped, toothed, and <u>sharp-pointed</u>, with either a long, slender point or a short, abrupt one. Leaves are alternate, and also basal on long petioles. Plant, 3-12″ tall, grows in damp, shady places. Foothills-Subalpine. *Viola canadensis* and *rugulosa,* Violet Family.

WHITE MARSH VIOLET—or Swamp Violet—is similar but its petals are all' white—may be purple-veined. Leaves are round, heart-shaped or kidney-shaped and have <u>rounded, not pointed tips</u>. The plant creeps over wet meadows or swamps. *Viola pallens.*

NOTES. Violets are related to the cultivated pansies.

Unlike other plants, the attractive violet blossoms often do not produce seeds. The flowers that usually do produce violet seeds lack the colored petals, or never open, or may mature underground, coming up only after the seeds are ripe. They are self-pollinated. In many cases the seeds are dispersed by ants.

ALPINE SPRING-BEAUTY or Big-rooted Spring-beauty *(p. 101)*	5 separated petals. 3/4″ flowers have <u>red veins</u>. <u>Only 2 sepals</u>. <u>All leaves basal</u>, broad, fleshy, entire. Plant 1-4″. Chiefly alpine.

The blossoms often form an attractive ring circling the leaf rosette. The glossy leaf edges may be touched with red and they grow in a basal rosette 1-1/2 to 6″ wide. Plant prefers rocky nooks, often above 12,000 feet. It is sometimes called Big-rooted Spring-beauty because of its exceptionally large, purple taproot. *Claytonia megarhiza,* Purslane Family.

See SPRING-BEAUTY or Water Spring-Beauty in Red/Saucer	Flower about 1/2″ wide, 5 veined petals but only 2 sepals. Opposite leaves, entire. Is either: 1) an early spring plant or 2) a plant creeping in wet places.

MOUSE-EAR CHICKWEED *(p. 102)* *(color plate p. 53)*	1/2″ erect flowers. 5 slit petals look like 10, with rounded tips. Inner petal base green. Small, opposite leaves. Prefers dry places.

Pale shading on the petal bases provides a dainty green background for the yellow-tipped stamens. Leaves are pointed and slightly downy, hence the name "Mouse-ear." Stems are 3-12″ tall. Chickweed is widely distributed, growing in dry fields and open meadows in all zones, Apr.-Aug. *Cerastium arvense,* Pink Family.

ALPINE MOUSE-EAR—has similar flowers but is a low, matted plant found only at high altitudes. *Cerastium beeringianum,* Pink Family.

ALP-LILY *(p. 102)*	One star flower tops each slender stem. 6 veined lobes, yellowish-green at base. Grass-like leaves. Plant 2-6″ tall. Chiefly alpine.

Plant has only a few delicate leaves like fine grass, and is usually found on exposed, rocky slopes. *Lloydia serotina,* Lily Family.

ALPINE SANDWORT or Arctic Sandwort *(p. 102)* *(color plate p. 53)*	5 rounded petals with greenish veins and bases. Fine, mossy mat usually about 1″ high. Chiefly alpine.

Petals are separated at the ends and are sometimes notched. They taper towards the greenish bases. Plant is a green cushion, 1/2 to 2″ high and from 2-30″ across, covered with many little, starlike flowers. It is abundant on sandy or rocky ground above timberline. *Arenaria obtusiloba,* Pink Family.

NOTE. "Wort" comes from Wyrt, the old English word for "plant."

FENDLER SANDWORT *(p. 102)*	5 petals. 1/3″ flowers. Red-tipped stamens look like dots against the "squared-off" petals. Leaves opposite, wiry, grass-like.

The star-like flowers have 10 stamens that look like red dots against the white petals. Tiny sepals are green and pointed. Plant is tufted, 3-12″ tall, and grows on dry hillsides and under pines. Foothills-Alpine. *Arenaria fendleri,* Pink Family.

STARWORT	1/4" flower with 10 pointed lobes (actually 5 deeply-slit petals.) Thread-like, square stem. Opposite grass-like leaves. In damp places.
(p. 102)	

The petals have pointed, star-like tips. Sometimes little dark-tipped stamens dot the white petals. Leaves are 1/2 to 4" long. The delicate stem is square, not round (not easy to see this), and is 2-12" tall. It grows near water. Foothills-Montane. *Stellaria longipes, longifolia* and others, Pink Family.

DRUMMOND ROCK-CRESS	4 petals. Small flat flowers, single or in clusters. Few waxy, narrow, alternate leaves with "ears" at base. Pods like big needles stand up erect beside stem.
(See Red/Saucer)	

MICROSTERIS	5 flat, notched petals. Tiny whitish flowers. Lower leaves opposite, narrow. Tiny plant, is easily missed.
(p. 102)	

Flowers are white or pink-tinged; have a tiny tube. Leaves may be reddish beneath. Plant 1-4" high, is common but inconspicuous. Plains-Foothills; Colo. to Mont. *Microsteris gracilis,* Phlox Family.

White Evening-star

Prickly Poppy

**White Stemless
Evening-primrose**

**Nuttall
Evening-primrose**

Mariposa

White Geranium

Narcissus Anemone

White Marsh-Marigold

Sand-lily

Field Bindweed

Cut-leaf Evening-primrose

Mountain Dryad

Wood-nymph

Mountain Phlox

Wild Strawberry

Alpine Spring-beauty

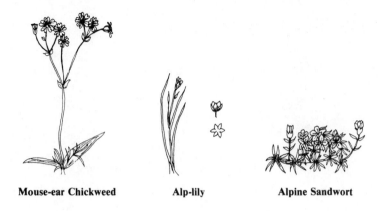

Mouse-ear Chickweed　　　**Alp-lily**　　　**Alpine Sandwort**

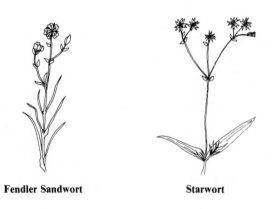

Fendler Sandwort　　　　　**Starwort**

Microsteris

WHITE CAMPION
or Evening Campion
(p. 104)

> 5 slit petals. Saucer flower with large inflated, ribbed calyx 5/8″ long. Opposite leaves, entire, veined. Knobby stems 1-2′ tall.

The conspicuous calyx has 10 stripes or ribs. From its end, the petals spread out with V-shaped slits. Flowers open at night and close the next day. They are white—rarely pinkish—and may be erect or nodding. Narrow leaves are 1-4″ long. Branched stems. On fields and roadsides, Foothills-Montane. Most common in Colo. *Lychnis alba,* Pink Family.

KINNIKINNIK
or Bearberry
(p. 104)

> 1/4″ pink and white, jug-like flowers hang among leaves on low mat in dry woods. Alternate leaves, entire, shiny, leathery.

5 petals. The little jugs are usually white with pink tips and they nod on curved stems; are partly hidden among the small, evergreen leaves. This is a prostrate shrub 2-5″ high, and very common on dry, rocky ground in open woods. Foothills-Montane. *Arctostaphylos uva-ursi,* Heath Family.

NOTES. Kinnikinnik is circumpolar. The bright red berries, sometimes called "chipmunk's apples", are much relished by all birds, and by bears and rodents. Uva-ursi means, "bearberry". During winter, they are a good source of food for deer and mountain sheep. Indians and early settlers ate the berries and used the leaves as a tobacco adulterant. We use them in medicine. The leaves also contain tannin, used in curing pelts.

ALPINE LANTERNS

> 5 very short petals. Large calyxes have 10 stripes. Flowers hang down. Alpine. Under 4″.

Flowers white—may be purplish—and look like Chinese lanterns. Colo. and Utah north, and circumpolar. *Lychnis apetala,* Pink Family.

Kinnikinnik

White Campion

Orchid Penstemon
(p. 113)

Parry Gentian
(p. 126)

Tansy-aster
(p. 109)

Showy Loco
(p. 118)

Colorado Columbine
(p. 135)

Wild Blue Flax
(p. 130)

Harebell
(p. 137)

Alpine Lousewort
(p. 116-117)

Tall Chiming Bells
(p. 121)

Nelson   Larkspur
(p. 114)

Sugar-bowl
(p. 136)

Chicory
(p. 129)

Tall Penstemon
(p. 113)

Purple Pincushion
(p. 121)

Silvery Lupine
(p. 120)

Alpine Phlox
(p. 132)

SUBALPINE DAISY
(p. 112)

> 1-2″ flower. 30 to 80 rays 1/8 to 3/16″ wide, and lavender to rose-purple. Yellow center. Bracts curl back. Basal leaves larger and have petioles. Prefers damp places. Stems erect.

Usually 1 showy head to a stem; sometimes 2 or 3. The rays are very wide for a daisy but flower has the daisy bracts—see Key Terms. They end in loose, pointed tips. The few upper leaves often clasp the stem. The plant varies greatly in height but is generally 12-15″. Common among evergreens and in meadows, usually in damp soil. Chiefly subalpine. *Erigeron peregrinus,* Composite Family.

SHOWY TOWNSENDIA
(See Red/Daisy Shape)

> 1-2″ rose-purple flower, greenish-yellow center. Rays are grooved. Leaves gray, grass-like. One to several 2-8″ stems.

SHOWY DAISY
or Showy Erigeron,
or Aspen Erigeron,
or Showy Fleabane.

> 1-2″ flowers have 75 to 150 narrow rays, usually lavender. Yellow center. Tiny hairs on leaf edges. Most leaves about the same size.

Very narrow rays circle a center of tightly packed, yellow disk flowers; like lavender fringe around a golden button. Often the rays are so thick that they appear to be in 2 layers. Color sometimes varies from blue to violet. There are 1 to 10 flowers on each stem, and the bracts usually have long hairs. Leaves, alternate and entire, are generally longer than the distance between their bases. The basal leaves are petioled. Plant often has several 1-2′ stems, and it grows along roadsides and on open rocky places. This is the most common daisy of the montane zone—also found in subalpine. *Erigeron speciosus,* Composite Family.

The ASPEN-DAISY—the common Colorado variety of the above, has no long hairs on the bracts, the stems usually lean somewhat, and the plant grows in aspen groves and meadows. *Erigeron speciosus*—var. *macranthus,* Composite Family. *(p. 112)*

TANSY-ASTER
(p. 112)
(color plate p. 105)

> Numerous flowers with purple rays and orange centers. Bracts are sticky and curve down. Branched plant along roadsides.

Flowers have beautiful purple or reddish-purple rays. Leaves are variable; usually sharply and irregularly toothed. One similar species has divided leaves. Plant has rough stems much branched near the top, is sticky, and has a characteristic, pungent odor. Very common in late summer (Aug.-Oct.), blooming profusely in fields and along roads where it forms a rich purple border. *Machaeranthera bigelovii,* or *Aster bigelovii,* Composite Family.

PRAIRIE CONEFLOWER (See Yellow/Daisy Shape)	Cylindrical cone 1/2 to 1-1/2″ long (or more), on long stalk. 3 to 7 purplish, wide rays at base of cone. Leaves much cut. Plant 1 to 2-1/2′. Dry plains.

ONE-FLOWERED DAISY or One-flowered Erigeron (er IJ er on) *(p. 112)*	Single 1″ flower on each stem. Blue or purplish rays, yellow center. Bracts have woolly hair. Entire leaves. Plant 1-8″.

The rays are narrow and very thick. Flower is often darker around the edge of the yellow disk center. The bracts have dark tips and are quite woolly with long white or gray or brownish-purple hairs. Leaves are mostly basal. Plant is common around lakes and on mountain tops. Chiefly alpine. *Erigeron simplex,* Composite Family.

PINNATE-LEAF DAISY *(p. 112)*	1″ flower has blue to purple rays and yellowish center. Bracts often purplish on edges. Tiny, lobed leaflets along each side of petiole. Plant 1-5″.

The dark flower bracts curl back slightly. Leaves on the stem are very small; the basal leaves are narrow and fernlike. Plant often grows in clumps. Subalpine-Alpine. Found chiefly on tundra, Wyo. to New Mex. *Erigeron pinnatisectus,* Compostie Family.

There are many species of both asters and daisies in the Rocky Mountains. H.D. Harrington, in his "Manual of the Plants of Colorado" lists 36 species of asters and 36 of erigerons (daisies). Many of these are very difficult to identify. Also some flowers that are not erigerons, are commonly called daisies.

7 Asters and 13 Daisies are included in this book. For distinctions between Daisies and Asters see Key Terms or Glossary.

BLUE ASTERS *(p. 112)*	Flowers about 1″, usually several on each stem. Have blue rays (or rose-purple); yellow centers and <u>aster bracts</u>. Leaves alternate, narrow; upper ones may clasp stem. Mostly Jul-Oct; 3 common species are:

1. **SMOOTH ASTER**—Flowers are usually numerous and <u>usually bright blue</u>. Leaves. 2-8″ long, are toothed; upper ones <u>clasp stem with little wings</u>. No hair—except sometimes minute hairs along the edge of the leaves.
   This is a common fall aster, 1-3′ tall, blooming in moist locations. Foothills-Montane. From the Rockies eastward. *Aster laevis,* Composite Family.
2. **PACIFIC ASTER**—Flowers, few to many, are <u>usually pale blue</u>. May be lavender or pinkish. Leaves are entire. Plant is much branched at top, is slightly to densely hairy, is generally in clumps, and is very common. Foothills-Subalpine. *Aster chilensis* or *adscendens.*
3. **SUN-LOVING ASTER**—Flowers have violet or bright rose rays. The bracts are loose and leaf-like, often with purple edges. Unlike most asters, this one may have only a few flowers; often just one. Leaves are numerous. The lower ones are mostly entire with petioles. The <u>2-8″ stems</u> are <u>decumbent</u>. Subalpine-Alpine *Aster foliaceous,* var. *apricus.*

NOTE. The name, "Aster" comes from the Greek word, <u>aster,</u> meaning "star.".

SPREADING DAISY or Branching Erigeron *(p. 112)*	<u>Many 3/4″ flowers,</u> yellow center, very narrow rays. Narrow leaves. <u>Many spreading stems</u> usually under 12″. Sandy soil. <u>Stem hairs spread out.</u>

Flowers are pale purple, to pinkish to white. Leaves are alternate, hairy and entire—or coarsely toothed. Plant is much branched from the base with rather woody stems, 4-24″. It is hairy and the stem hairs spread straight out instead of resting against the stem. Plant grows along roadsides and on sandy ground. Plains-Foothills. May-Sep. *Erigeron divergens,* Composite Family.

CUT-LEAF DAISY (See White/Daisy Shape)	1/2″ flower, bluish rays, yellow center. Leaves divided into 3's once or twice. Plant 2-6″. Dry places.

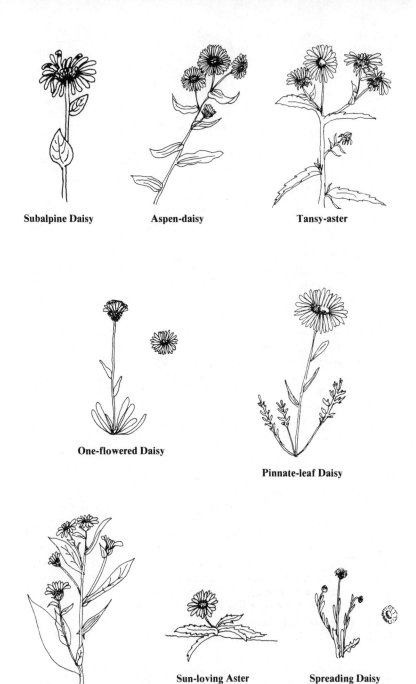

Subalpine Daisy

Aspen-daisy

Tansy-aster

One-flowered Daisy

Pinnate-leaf Daisy

Smooth Aster

Sun-loving Aster

Spreading Daisy

PENSTEMON
or Beardtongue
(p. 123)
(color plate p. 105, 108)

Tube flowers 3/4 to 1-1/2″, open out into 2 lips (see Key Terms). Flowers are usually all on one side of stem. Leaves are opposite and usually entire. Stems unbranched.

The many species of penstemon are among our most beautiful wildflowers, presenting colorful displays in blue, purple, lavender, and red.

Penstemons—the word means 5 stamens—have 5 stamens but only 4 of them function. The fifth has no anther (the pollen-producing organ). Its tip may be smooth or may have a little tuft of hair at the end or along its side. Hence, the common name of "Beardtongue."

Penstemons grow in sandy, rocky soil. The flower throat is abruptly expanded. And the color is extremely variable, ranging from pink or whitish to deep purple. Some species have large flowers; others have small ones. 5 common, large-flowered species are:

1. **ORCHID PENSTEMON or ORCHID or PURPLE BEARD-TONGUE or SIDEBELLS PENSTEMON**—Flowers are—usually—orchid or lilac. Very showy. Always on one side of stem. Flower throat flares open showing dark yellow hair on the sterile stamen. Leaves are broader at base, clasping stem. They are entire, pointed, waxy, firm and bluish or blue-gray. Plant has sturdy 4-16″ stems and blooms in spring. Foothills-Montane. Wyo.-New Mex. *Penstemon secondiflorus,* Figwort Family.

2. **TALL PENSTEMON**—Flowers are—usually—blue, light blue, pinkish or lavender, and are on one side of stem; sometimes in sets of 3 or more. Upper lip is arched-erect, the lower one spreads down. Plant has one to many stout, 8-30″ stems (rarely taller) with narrow, entire leaves. Stem often curves upward slightly from base. Blooms in summer. Foothills-Montane. Wyo. to New Mex. and Ariz. *Penstemon unilateralis—virgata.*

3. **ALPINE PENSTEMON or MTN. BEARDTONGUE**—Showy flowers on one side of stem are—usually—bright azure blue. Lower lip spreads downwards. Leafy bracts below the flowers. Leaves are entire and deep green. Plant has stout stems 6-12″ (rarely taller); often in clumps, and grows from Wyo. southward. Foothills-Alpine. *Penstemon alpinus.*

4. **DARK or WHIPPLE PENSTEMON**—Flowers—usually—are either very dark wine or dull purple; almost black. A dull white form of this species often grows with the purple ones. Flowers bloom in loose rows around the stem or in a head-like cluster. Lower lip of flower projects beyond the upper. Leaves entire or

113

toothed; upper ones clasp stem. Plant, 4-28″, grows on wooded slopes or gravelly soil. Montane-Alpine. Ida. and Wyo. to Ariz. and New Mex. *Penstemon whippleanus.*

5. **HALLS ALPINE PENSTEMON**—Flowers are reddish—or bluish-purple to violet, with white markings at the throat which is abruptly inflated like a 2-lipped bell flower. Flowers along stem or in small clusters. Little or no hair in flower throat. Leaves are oblanceolate or linear, and entire. Usually several sturdy 4-8″ stems rise from tufts of leaves. Plant is alpine and grows chiefly in Colo. *Penstemon hallii.*

GENTIANS (See Blue/Head)	Erect, cup-shaped flowers 1-2″ deep; purple to blue. 4 or 5 petals spread out from lip of cup (or turn up). Leaves opposite, entire.
MONKSHOOD *(p. 123)*	1″ bluish-purple, hooded flowers. 2 lobes at base, 2 larger lobes at sides, and on top is a "peaked hood." Deeply cut leaves. Moist ground.

The helmet-like flowers (rarely white) are sparsely scattered along the top part of the stalk. Sepals and petals are about the same color and one large sepal comes forward to form a peaked cap over the flower, ending in a sharp point in front—supposedly like caps worn by medieval monks. The lower petals have white streaks with purple veins. Leaves, 2-6″ wide, are alternate and dark green. Plant, 2-5′ tall, grows along streams and in wet places. Montane-Subalpine. Jun.-Sep. *Aconitum columbianum,* Buttercup Family.

NOTE. Monkshoods are poisonous. They contain the alkaloids, aconitine and aconine, especially in the roots and seeds. The drug, aconite, obtained from this plant is a heart sedative.

LARKSPUR *((p. 123)* *(color plate p. 107)*	3/4″ purple—or blue—flowers with spur. 4 petals in a knot; 5 colored sepals. Divided leaves. 5 species are:

1. **NELSON LARKSPUR**—Dark blue to rich purple, spurred flowers bloom along an erect stem. The top sepal extends backwards or sideways in a tube-like spur 1″ long. Leaves are circular in outline but deeply cut into narrow parts. Only a few stem leaves. Plant, 4-20″ tall, grows in either sunny or shady places. Foothills-Montane. Apr.-Jun. *Delphinium nelsonii,* Buttercup Family.

2. **GEYER LARKSPUR**—Flowers like the above only they are bright blue. Leaves and stems are hairy, and the plant is 8-28″.

It grows in Utah, Wyo. and Colo. to Nebr. and is very poisonous to livestock. *Delphinium geyeri.*

3. **SUBALPINE LARKSPUR**—has rich, dark purple flowers like Nelson Larkspur, but flower clusters are crowded; upper petals are edged with white; usually has 6 to 20 leafy stems, 3-6' tall. Plant blooms Jul.-Aug. in wet subalpine meadows and bogs. Wyo. and Utah. *Delphinium barbeyii.*

4. **TALL MTN. LARKSPUR**—Flowers are bright blue to light purplish—are not crowded. Petal edges are not white but sepals may be dull gray on back. Stem bases may be straw-colored; plant is 3-6' tall, and blooms Jul.-Aug. in meadows and woods. Montane-Subalpine. Colo. to Mont. and Ida. *Delphinium occidentale, ramosum,* and others

5. **PLAINS LARKSPUR**—Flowers are pale blue to whitish. Stems are 1-3'. Plains-Foothills. Colo. south. *Delphinium virescens.*

GIANT HYSSOP	2-lipped flowers with 1/2″ tube; purple to white, in dense <u>terminal</u> clusters 2-6″ long. Leaves opposite, toothed. Square stems 2-6'.

Large flower clusters at ends of stout, leafy stems. Leaves ovate to triangular-ovate. Grows in moist soil in valleys and slopes. Montane-Subalpine. *Agastache urticifolia,* Mint Family.

CHICORY (See Blue/Saucer)	Bright blue flowers of rays only (look like a dandelion). Most leaves basal; one small leaf or bract at base of each branch. Much <u>branched stem,</u> 1-4'.

SKULLCAP *(p. 123)*	Purplish, 2-lipped flowers in pairs (a single flower in each axil of opposite, upper leaves.) Calyx forms a small cap on top of flower. On open, dry slopes.

Flowers stand erect in leaf axils. The lower lip is wide-spread with white streaks; upper lip is folded above a small throat, into a slender, pointed cap or crest. Leaves are narrow, 1-2″ long, and entire. Plant, 2-10″ tall, has square stems and it grows on hills and valleys. Foothills-Montane. Wyo.-New Mex. *Scutellaria brittoni,* Mint Family.

STAR GENTIAN *(p. 123)*	3/4″ purplish-blue star flowers; pointed petals. No tubes. Leaves chiefly basal, entire. Erect plant in <u>wet places.</u>

Flowers are wide open stars, inky blue to purple with 4 to 6 petals—usually 5. Basal leaves long; smaller ones on stem, alternate or opposite. Plant is 4-16″ tall. Subalpine-Alpine. Colo. to Canada; and in northern mountains around the world. *Swertia perennis,* Gentian Family.

JAMES SAXIFRAGE (See Red/Stalk)	Clusters of rose-purple flowers. 5 "clawed" petals, with wide spaces at their base. Leaves alternate, rounded and scalloped. In rock crevices.

JACOBS LADDER *(p. 123)*	5 petals. Clusters of 3/4″ funnel-shaped flowers, light blue to purplish-blue. Alternate leaves; many leaflets. Stems leaning or erect. Crushed leaves smell bad but the flowers are sweetly fragrant. 3 species are:

1. **DELICATE JACOBS LADDER**—Loose clusters of 1/2″ flowers, usually sky-blue and very dainty. Leaves, mostly basal, are fern-like with 11 to 23 thin, pale green leaflets, usually in pairs, suggesting a ladder. The branched stems, 1 foot or less, are weak and spreading or leaning and often grow in clumps in spruce forests or under twisted trees at timberline. Subalpine-Alpine. Ida. and Wyo. south. *Polemonium delicatum,* Phlox Family.
2. **LEAFY JACOBS LADDER**—Light blue to purplish blue flowers are in thick, flat-topped clusters about 2″ wide. The 12 to 25 leaflets are broad, hairy, and crowded. Plant, 1-3′ tall, is hairy, very leafy, and much branched—almost bushy. On meadows, slopes and along roads. Foothills-Montane. *Polemonium foliosissimum.*
3. **WESTERN JACOBS LADDER**—Flowers like the preceding but the clusters are longer than wide. Leaflets are narrow, non-hairy and not crowded. Upper leaves are smaller than the lower ones. Plant has slender, unbranched stems and grows in moist meadows. Montane-Subalpine. Colo., Utah and Calif. north to the Arctic. *Polemonium caeruleum or occidentale.*

PURPLE LOUSEWORT *(p. 123)* *(color plate p. 106)*	3/4″, 2-lipped flowers with lower lip spreading; upper lip compressed on the sides and strongly arched. Leaves narrow, alternate and basal, scalloped.* In wet places.

Striking, rosy-purplish flowers are densely crowded along the spike. Leaves are 1/2 to 1-1/2″ long with scalloped edges. Plant, about 1 foot tall, is found in mountain meadows. Montane-Subalpine. Colo. to Wyo. to Nev. *Pedicularis crenulata,* Figwort Family.

*ALPINE LOUSEWORT or ROCKY MOUNTAIN LOUSEWORT—Flowers are like those of Purple Lousewort, but the leaves are divided into narrow parts like a comb; the divisions not reaching quite to the midrib. Subalpine-Alpine. Montana to Colo. Rather rare. *Pedicularis sudetica,* var. *scopulorum.*

MILKVETCH *(p. 123)*	Clusters of 1/4 to 1″ pea flowers with a blunt keel (see Key Terms). Alternate leaves with many small, entire, pinnate leaflets. No tendrils. 3 common purple milkvetches follow.

All Milkvetches have pea flowers with blunt or rounded keels. The flowers are purple or white (rarely yellowish), and most are on erect or ascending, leafy, branched stems.

There are several dozen species of Milkvetch in the Rocky Mtns. and many of them are difficult even for botanists to distinguish. Positive identification of most can be made only by technical points but 6 of those easiest to identify have been included in this book.

1. **EARLY PURPLE MILKVETCH**—The 1″, rose-purple flowers bloom in crowded clusters. Leaflets are ovate and silky-hairy. The stems are about 4″ long. This is common in early spring—Apr–May. Plains-Foothills. Wyo. to New Mex. The 1-2″ pods are curved and leathery—may be fleshy at first. *Astragalus shortianus,* Pea Family.

2. **TWO-GROOVED MILKVETCH**—Numerous flowers are purple to rose-purple (rarely whitish) and usually bend down. Leaflets are ovate to linear-oblong. The 1-3′ stems are erect, and grow on dry soil. Plains-Foothills. The 1/2″ pods have 2 grooves on the upper surface. This milkvetch and some others often grow on soil containing selenium, in which case they become very poisonous to livestock. *Astragalus bisulcatus.*

3. **ALPINE MILKVETCH**—The 1/2″ flowers are two-toned (purple and bluish or whitish). The keel is as long as the banner, and the calyx is covered with black hairs. The pods are black-hairy, and hang down. Leaflets are oval and notched at the tip. Stems, 4-12″ long, are decumbent. This dainty plant is common in forests; Montane-Alpine. It is found in northern and mountainous regions of North America, Europe and Asia. *Astragalus alpinus.*

LAMBERT LOCO
(See Red/Stalk)

> Pea flowers with <u>sharp</u> beak (see Key Terms). Showy, rose-purple, on leafless stems. Leaves have many silvery leaflets <u>in pairs</u>; <u>or nearly so.</u>

SHOWY LOCO
or Whorl-leaf Loco
(p. 123)
(color plate p. 105)

> 1/2" rosy-purple pea flowers with sharp beak, on soft, silvery-woolly stems 8-14" tall. Lower buds open first. Leaves have many leaflets whorled in 4's or 3's.

Buds and beautiful magenta or purple flowers cover the top section of silky-hairy spikes. Most of the leaflets are whorled; i.e., circling the midrib in rows of 4 each (sometimes 3). Leaves are basal and very silvery. *Oxytropis splendens,* Pea Family.

May be either
AMERICAN VETCH
or PURPLE PEAVINE

> 3/4" purple pea flowers in axillary clusters. Very narrow leaflets; <u>fine</u> <u>tendrils.</u> Square stems. <u>Vines.</u>

AMERICAN VETCH
(p. 124)

> Cluster of a <u>few</u> 3/4", light purple to deep purple flowers. Leaves end in tendrils.

Delicate vine, climbing or trailing; never erect. Plains-Montane. Blooms in spring. *Vicia americana,* Pea Family.

PURPLE PEAVINE
or Wild Sweet Pea

> 1" rose-purple flowers, single or in long clusters. Upper leaves end in tendrils; lower ones may end in bristles. Vine may be erect, climbing, or trailing.

Colo. and Utah south. Plains-Montane. *Lathyrus eucosmus,* Pea Family.

One definite distinction between these two is in the style—best seen with a lens. American vetch has a slender style with a tuft of hairs at or near the tip. Purple Peavine's style is hairy along one side but has no tuft.

NOTE. The cultivated sweet pea belongs to the Lathyrus genus.

BLUE MIST
  PENSTEMON
or Low Penstemon

(p. 124)

> 1/2", 2-lipped flower (see Key Terms). Usually deep blue. Leaves opposite. Several stems 4-10" (or 14"). Gravelly, wooded slopes.

This is one of the small-flowered penstemons. Color varies from light to dark blue; and it may bloom on only one side of the stem, or all around it. Leaves, bright green and shiny, may or may not be toothed. Plant has several stems, often in clumps. It is called Blue Mist because it sometimes blooms so densely along slopes as to give them a misty blue appearance from a distance. Foothills-Subalpine. Along the Eastern Slope in Colo. and Wyo. *Penstemon virens,* Figwort Family. A similar species (*Penstemon humilis*) with duller, entire leaves grows from N.W. Colo. and Wyo. to Ida. and Calif.

CLUSTERED
  PENSTEMON

(p. 124)

> Purple cluster of 1/3" tube flowers at top of stem; below are usually from 1 to 4 separate rows of flowers circling stem. Leaves opposite and basal.

Flowers are arranged in rows or rings of up to 25. Each ring is well separated from the one below it. The flowers usually tilt down. This is the common form of the plant, but sometimes it occurs without any rings—just one flower cluster at top of stem. Leaves are entire and bright green; may be shiny. The stems are generally 4-12" tall, and grow in moist places often covering large areas. Montane-Alpine. Colo. to Alaska. *Penstemon procerus,* Figwort Family.

VENUS LOOKING
  GLASS

(p. 124)

> 5 petals. 1/2" flat flowers in the cup-like axils of short, broad, alternate, scalloped leaves that clasp the stout stem.

Flowers are blue to purplish; usually bluish-lavender, and the stamens protrude from a 1/4" tube. Leaves are bluish-green and broadly heart-shaped. By clasping the stem they form small cups for the flowers; usually one flower in each cup. Plant generally has a single, sturdy, leafy, unbranched stem 6-20" tall, and angled—not round. Grows on dry slopes and on grasslands. Foothills-Montane. *Triodanis perfoliata,* Bellflower Family.

LUPINE

(p. 124)

(color plate p. 108)

1/4" to 1/2" pea flowers (see Key Terms) along erect stalk. 5 to 11 entire, palmate leaflets radiate from the tip of petiole. Hairy, bushy plant. 6 species are:

A. Lupines 1-3' tall with flowers higher than the leaves.

1. **SILVERY LUPINE**—1/2" flowers are light or dark blue to purple; may even be bi-colored. Have purple veins. The long, narrow leaflets are all attached to the tip of the petiole and may be silvery or dull green. The rather woody stems, 12-40" tall, are much branched, and grow either in the open or in partial shade. Foothills-Subalpine. *Lupinus argenteus,* Pea Family.

   NOTE. TEXAS BLUEBONNET *Lupinus subcarnosus,* is similar to the above, and is the state flower of Texas.

2. **LODGEPOLE LUPINE**—is very similar to Silvery Lupine but the 1/4" flowers range from purple or dark blue to dingy white, turning brown as they fade. Most common in the montane zone. *Lupinus parviflorus.*

3. **NEBRASKA LUPINE**—Flowers, over 1/2" long, are blue with a purple spot on the banner. Common among sagebrush. Plains-Foothills, especially on the plains. *Lupinus plattensis.*

B. Lupines usually less than 10" tall, with leaves as high or higher than the flowers:

4. **KINGS LUPINE**—usually has dark blue flowers, and leaflets silky-hairy on both sides. West of the Continental Divide from Utah and Colo. south. Plains-Foothills. *Lupinus kingii.* *(p. 124)*

5. **LOW LUPINE**—Flowers purplish to almost white. Stems have stiff, gray hairs, and are decumbent. Plains-Foothills. East of the Continental Divide. *Lupinus pusillus.*

6. **CUSHION LUPINE**—1/4" flowers, pale blue or lavender, are partly buried in the leaves which form a mat or cushion less than 6" high. 1/2" leaflets are silky-hairy. Montane zone from central Colo. to Mont. *Lupinus lepidus* var. *utahensis.*

NOTE. The word, lupine, comes from "lupus", wolf, because it was once believed that lupines robbed the soil. Now we know that bacteria on their roots are able to take nitrogen from the air and make plant food. So these plants and other members of the pea family, enrich the soil instead of robbing it.

CHIMING BELLS	5 petals. Clusters of 3/8″ bell flowers
(p. 124)	hang down. May or may not have
(color plate p. 107)	pink buds. Leaves entire, alternate. Plant 3″ to 3-1/2′. 3 common species are:

1. **LANCELEAF CHIMING BELLS or FOOTHILLS MERTEN-SIA or LANGUID LADY**—Dainty, little, light blue bells hang down in sprays, together with pinkish buds. Sometimes there are both blue and pink bells. Leaves are dull green or bluish. Usually a single 5-15″ stem that often leans. Common in spring in dry places. Plains-Montane. Later in the season the stems may be more delicate and the flowers small and very pale with only 3 or 4 bells in a spray. *Mertensia lanceolata,* Borage Family.

2. **TALL CHIMING BELLS or TALL MERTENSIA**—Flowers like the above. Leaves are green, fairly thick, broad, and veined. The stems, 1 to 3-1/2′ tall, are graceful, branching and leafy. Found in dense clumps along mountain streams or in damp, shady places. Montane-Alpine. *Mertensia ciliata.*

NOTE. Deer, elk, bears and domestic sheep graze on Tall Chiming Bells. At high altitudes, the pika (rock rabbit) cuts, dries and stores it for food during winter.

3. **ALPINE CHIMING BELLS or GREENLEAF MERTEN-SIA**—Flowers are like the preceding, but the sprays are deep blue, with little or no pink, and are fragrant. Plant has deep green leaves and stout stems; grows in leafy tufts 3-12″ high, on alpine tundra. Mont. to Colo. and Utah. *Mertensia viridis.*

LOVE GENTIAN	Rose-lavender star flower with 3/8″
(See Red/Stalk)	tube. 4 or 5 pointed petals. Fringe in flower throat. Leaves opposite, entire, sessile. Single stem 3-14″.

PURPLE PINCUSHION	1/4″ purple, cup-like flowers cover
or Purple Fringe	upper part of a 4-12″ spike. Gold-tipped stamens protrude. Gray, fern leaves, alternate.
(p. 124)	
(color plate p. 108)	

Flowers form a dense cone 2-4″ long from which the stamens of each little flower protrude with golden anthers so that the spike resembles a long, purple pincushion filled with gold-headed pins. The finely divided leaves are covered with silvery-silky hairs. The unbranched stems are often in clumps, growing on sandy, gravelly soil, especially along roads. Montane-Alpine. *Phacelia sericea,* Waterleaf Family.

COLLOMIA (See Red/Head)	Dense cluster of lavender trumpet flowers among leafy bracts. Leaves entire, usually alternate. Stem 2-12", often on sandy soil.

FALSE
   FORGET-ME-NOT
or Stickseed Forget-
   me-not *(p. 124)*
	5 petals. 1/4" saucer flowers in rounded clusters. Yellow-eye center. No bracts between flowers. Long, entire leaves. Erect plant 1-4'.

The blue to whitish petals and yellow-eye center look much like true forget-me-nots. This is called Stickseed because the small seeds or nutlets have rows of barbed prickles which can easily enter clothing or animal fur, thus providing the seeds with free transportation. Plant grows along roads, in aspen groves, and on mountainsides. Montane-Subalpine. *Hackelia floribunda.* Borage Family.

ALFALFA	Small heads of 1/3" purplish pea flowers. 3 leaflets, toothed near tips. Woody, square, green stems. Pods spirally coiled.

Flower heads are axillary, and stems are erect. This is cultivated for hay but often escapes to roadsides. *Medicago sativa,* Pea Family.

MOUNTAIN FORGET-ME-NOT	5 petals. Tiny, bright blue, saucer flowers along one side of stem. Crest in throat. Leaves alternate, entire. Stems 4-12".

Leaves narrow; hairy stems in dense cluster. Foothills-Alpine. Colo. north. *Myosotis alpestris,* Borage Family.

COMMON STICKSEED	5 petals. 1/8" pale blue to whitish, flat flowers. Leaflike bracts between flowers. Leaves alternate, entire.

Branches turn up. Leaves slightly rough. Prickly nutlets stick to clothing. Common in dry sandy places. Plains-Montane. *Lappula redowski,* Borage Family.

AMERICAN SPEEDWELL or American Brooklime	4 petals that drop easily. Flat flower blue to whitish. Leaves opposite, toothed. In water or wet places.

Plant weak, 4-24"; may be erect but is usually trailing. Plains-Subalpine, *Veronica americana,* Figwort Family.

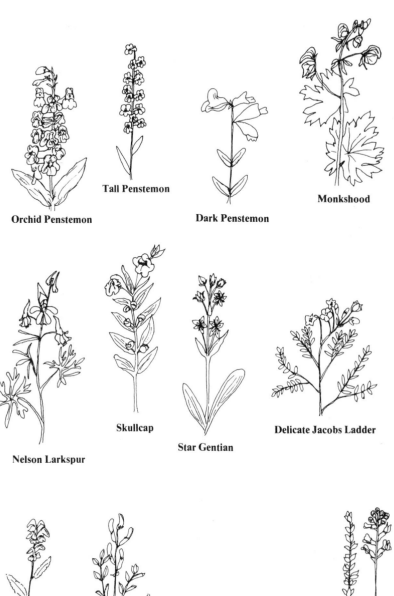

Tall Penstemon

Orchid Penstemon

Dark Penstemon

Monkshood

Skullcap

Star Gentian

Nelson Larkspur

Delicate Jacobs Ladder

Early Purple Milkvetch

Purple Lousewort

Alpine Milkvetch

Showy Loco

American Vetch

Blue Mist Penstemon

Clustered Penstemon

Venus Looking Glass

Silvery Lupine

Kings Lupine

Lanceleaf Chiming Bells

Purple Pincushion

False Forget-me-not

SKY PILOT
(p 128)

5 violet-blue petals. 2″ cluster of 3/4″ funnel-form flowers. Orange stamens. Many tiny, green, oval, whorled leaflets.* Plant 3 to 12″. Alpine.

The petals join in a rich purplish-blue tube from which rise gold-tipped stamens and a white 3-pronged pistil. *30 to 50 leaflets are spaced along the petiole in rows of about 4 each. Plant grows in rocky places and may or may not be erect. Chiefly Alpine. All polemonium leaves have a skunk-like smell when crushed; the flowers themselves, however, are sweetly fragrant. *Polemonium viscosum,* Phlox Family.

BULL THISTLE
(p. 128)

2″ rose-purple flower puff. Bracts both spiny and cobwebby. Leaves spiny-edged but woolly-hairy below. Spiny tissue runs down stem below each leaf. Very spiny plant, 2-5′.

Head is composed of disk flowers only. In thistles, these flowers are unusually long and are split into narrow divisions which give the flower a fluffy appearance. Head is often solitary on branch ends. Plains-Foothills. *Cirsium vulgare,* or *lanceolatum,* Composite Family.

BRISTLE THISTLE
(See Red/Head)

2″ pink to purple flower puff. Wide, sharp, projecting bracts. Prickly leaves green on both sides. Very spiny plant.

NOTE. Thistles are an emblem of Scotland. According to legend, Norsemen once invaded Scotland intending to capture an important castle. In the dark of night they removed their shoes to wade across the moat, but it was dry and thistles were growing there. When the barefooted soldiers stepped on thistles instead of into water, their cries of pain woke the Scottish guards and the Norsemen were defeated.

WAVY-LEAF THISTLE
(See Red/Head)

Large rose-purple flower puff on long stem. Bracts are green, spiny and tightly overlapped. Leaves gray-green above, paler below. Their bases clasp stem. Very spiny plant.

CANADA THISTLE or Creeping Thistle *(p. 128)*	Numerous tight, rose-purple flower puffs at stem ends—3/4" wide. <u>Firm, green, spiny bracts form a base 1" long</u>. Leaves <u>green both sides</u>. Very spiny plant.

Like all true thistles, the heads are of disk flowers only. This branched plant has many heads about half as big as the 3 preceding thistles. Common in fields and moist spots along roads; often grows in colonies. Plains-Foothills. Called Creeping Thistle because of its creeping underground rootstalk, it is one of our worst weeds, extremely difficult to eradicate. *Cirsium arvense,* Composite Family.

GENTIAN *(p. 128)* *(color plate p. 105)*	Erect, cup-shaped flowers 1-2" deep; purple to blue; 4 or 5 petals spread out from lip of cup. Leaves opposite, entire. Late Jul.-Sep. 3 common species are:

1. **ROCKY MOUNTAIN FRINGED GENTIAN**—The petals, each about 1/2" wide, are <u>fringed on their margins</u>. On cloudy days, they twist together in an erect column but in bright sunshine, they open out wide, showing the beautiful blue-purple color and the fringe along their tips and sides. One or more stems, 6-12" tall, are each tipped with a single flower. Buds are twisted. Plant grows in damp, sunny meadows, especially in the subalpine zone. *Gentiana elegans or thermalis,* Gentian Family.

NOTES. The Rocky Mountain Fringed Gentian was named the Yellowstone Park flower because it is so abundant there.
It is also the floral emblem of autumn.

2. **PARRY GENTIAN**—Flowers are <u>barrel- or goblet-shaped</u> with bright, deep blue petals that open wide in full sunshine. But if a cloud covers the sun they close immediately, showing <u>brown and dark greenish bands on the outside</u>. 1 to 6 flowers at the top of each stem.
   <u>This is one of the plaited gentians</u>; that is, between the petals are short plaits or folds of tissue ending in a small tooth (same color as petals.) Leaves, 3/4" wide but pointed, <u>partially envelope the flower clusters</u>. Several leafy stems 4-20" tall. This is the largest-flowered and probably the most common gentian. It grows in meadows and forests from Wyo. and Utah south. Montane-Subalpine. *Gentiana calycosa, or parryi. (p. 128)*
3. **PRAIRIE GENTIAN**——This, also, is a plaited gentian. The 1" cylindrical flowers are blue to purple, and are <u>both axillary and</u>

terminal. They open in bright sunlight but close when cloudy. Leaves are narrow. The several stems 4-12″, are decumbent. Unlike most gentians, it grows in dry fields. Foothills-Montane. *Gentiana affinis.*

NOTE. The name, "gentian," comes from King Gentius of Illyria in Eastern Europe, where gentians grew in profusion.

HORSEMINT (See Red/Head)	Crowded cluster of many slender tube flowers about 1-1/2″ long, each with 2 protruding stamens. Fragrant, opposite, toothed leaves. Square stems.

ROCKY MOUNTAIN BEE PLANT (See Red/Head)	4 petals. Large cluster of purplish-pink flowers; stamens protrude twice the length of petals. Narrow, alternate, 3-fingered leaves. Narrow, hanging pods.

WATERLEAF *(p. 128)*	5 petals. Round heads of cup flowers about 1/4″. Stamens protrude like a pincushion. Leaves twice pinnately divided. Long leaf stalks. Moist, shady places. 2 species are:

1. **BALL-HEAD WATERLEAF**—The dense heads of lavender to violet flowers—sometimes white—are shorter than the leaves. The 5 to 7 leaflets are much divided. The 4-16″ plant is gray-hairy and is found from Colo. north. Foothills-Montane. *Hydrophyllum capitatum,* Waterleaf Family.
2. **FENDLER WATERLEAF**—The cluster is rather loose and the flowers are usually white—may be pale blue to violet. Flower heads are taller than the leaves. Large, thin leaves have 9-13 pointed leaflets that are divided again. Plant, 1-3′ tall, grows from Wyo. and Utah to New Mex. *Hydrophyllum fendleri.*

SCORPION-WEED (See White/Stalk)	5 petals. 1/4″ whitish to purple cup flowers in clusters curved like a fiddle neck. Stamens protrude. Leaves alternate. Plant usually dusty-green, stiff-hairy.

127

ALPINE VERONICA
or Alpine Speedwell
(p. 128)

> 4 rounded petals. Small cluster of 1/3″ dark blue flowers. Leaves sessile, opposite. Damp places.

Deep blue flowers form a cluster at or around top of stem. Petals fall easily. Leaves are ovate to oblong; entire or toothed. Erect stem 4-16″. Montane-Alpine. *Veronica wormskjoldii,* Figwort Family.

One of two ONIONS
(See Red/Head)

> 6 lobes. Cluster—erect or drooping—of 1/4″ lavender-pink flowers. Stamens may or may not protrude. Few grass-like leaves.

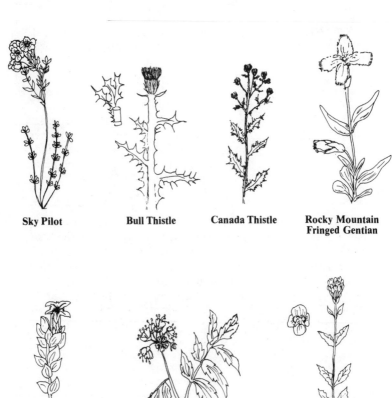

Sky Pilot   **Bull Thistle**   **Canada Thistle**   **Rocky Mountain Fringed Gentian**

Parry Gentian   **Fendler Waterleaf**   **Alpine Veronica**

PASQUE FLOWER or Anemone or Windflower *(p. 133)*	5 to 7 "petals." Lavender flower cup 1-1/2″ deep, blooms before furry leaves unfold. Large, leaf-like bracts circle stem 1-5″ below flower.

Anemones have no true petals but the pointed sepals look just like petals, and form a wide, upright cup. The inside is white to pale lavender; outside is dark lavender to purple, and silky-hairy. A leaf-like, furry involucre is wrapped around the bud but as the flower develops and pushes up, it leaves the involucre several inches below. Leaves come up and unfold after the plant has blossomed. They are silky-hairy and much divided, somewhat like deer antlers. Plant, 2-16″ tall, is one of our earliest spring flowers—Mar -Jun —and when emerging from the ground, looks like a fuzzy, little head. The seed plumes later are long and fluffy with delicate, very silky-shiny threads. Foothills-Subalpine. *Pulsatilla patens* or *Anemone patens,* Buttercup Family.

NOTES. This is the South Dakota state flower.

The word, "Pasque" comes from a French word meaning Easter. "Anemone" is from the Greek word, anemos, "wind;" the flowers were supposed to open at the command of the spring breezes.

The plant is used in medicine.

Pasque Flower is said to be one of the plants used to dye Easter eggs at the court of King Edward I, of England.

WILD GERANIUM (See Red/Saucer)	5 veined petals, separated. Lavender flowers with showy stamens. Usually are flat. Leaves deeply lobed. Hairy plant. Several to many stamens.

CHICORY *(p. 133)* *(color plate p. 107)*	1-1/4″ bright blue flowers of rays only (look like a blue dandelion). Most leaves basal; one small leaf or bract at base of each branch. Much branched stem, 1-4′.

The sky-blue rays are toothed at the square end. (Flowers may rarely be pink or white.) At the base of each ray is a little style with 2 stigmas that look like 2 tiny branches, curving downwards. This is characteristic, of course, of all rays in composites. The rays in the center of Chicory flowers are shorter than those around the outside. Basal leaves are long and toothed or lobed. The woody stem is grooved, and may become purplish-red. Because the leaves are so small, the many branches look almost bare. Chicory has milky juice. It grows along roads and in fields—prefers damp places. Plains-Foothills. *Cichorium intybus,* Composite Family.

NOTE. Like the dandelion, chicory was introduced from Europe. It is used in salad greens and the long roots serve as a coffee substitute.

BLUE LETTUCE (p. 133)	3/4″ flowers are light blue to violet, of rays only (look like a blue dandelion). Many stem leaves 2-8″ long; some are lobed. Unbranched stem, 1 to 3-1/2′.

Rays are toothed. Leaves are alternate and variable. Plant is nonhairy, and has milky sap. *Lactuca pulchella,* Composite Family.

OYSTER PLANT	Single flower of rays only, like a purplish dandelion; bracts are longer than the rays. Leaves grasslike and clasping at base.

When cooked, it tastes like oysters. Escaped from cultivation. Its seed head resembles those of dandelions. Plains-Foothills. *Tragopogon porrifolius,* Composite Family.

WILD BLUE FLAX or Lewis Flax (p. 134) (color plate p. 106)	5 rounded petals with purple lines. 1-1/4″ sky-blue flowers. Many leaves, alternate, narrow, short. Slender, swaying stems.

These beautiful, fragile flowers bloom on stems that sway in the slightest breeze. They open wide in the morning but wither under a hot sun. The slender but tough stems are 8″ to 2′ tall. Plains-Montane. *Linum Lewisii,* Flax Family.

NOTES. This species was named Lewisii for the leader of the Lewis and Clark Expedition, and these flowers grow over most of the western land explored by that party. Are also found from Alaska south to New Mex. and Calif.

Blue Flax has long, tough, stringy fibers because it belongs to the Flax Family from which linen thread and cloth are made. Indians used these fibers for making baskets, fishing nets, snowshoes, etc. Much of the wrapping around Egyptian mummies was made from flax. Linen, today, comes from cultivated flax. Linseed oil, obtained from flax seed, is used in paints, varnishes, and medicine.

SPIDERWORT **or Spiderlily** *(p. 134)*	3 petals. 1-1/4″ purple or rich blue flower, usually flat. 3 small, pointed, green sepals. Yellow tips on hairy stamens. Long, grass-like leaves.

Flower blooms in the forenoon. Leaves sheathe the stem and often stick out at odd angles. Plant, 6-18″, grows on rocky slopes and has a slimy juice. Plains-Montane. *Tradescantia occidentalis,* Spiderwort Family.

NOTES. It is probably called Spiderwort because of the cobwebby stamens, suggestive of spiders' legs.

The botanical name honors the Tradescants, father and son, who were gardeners for King Charles I of England, before he was beheaded. The son made several trips to the new colony of Virginia to study plants.

BLUE VIOLETS *(p. 134)*	5 slightly irregular petals. Bluish-purple flower nearly flat. There is a crook in the stem neck. The lowest petal turns backward to form a spur. 3 common species are:

1. **MOUNTAIN BLUE VIOLET or SUBALPINE BLUE VIOLET**—Because of the crook in its stem the flower nods slightly (typical of violets.) The 3/4″ flower is blue to violet-purple, and its slender spur is about 1/2 as long as the petals. Leaves are broadly ovate. The stem is 2-10″ but early in the season it may be very short. Plant grows along streams and moist places and is the most common blue summer violet of the higher zones. Foothills-Timberline. *Viola adunca,* Violet Family.

    A smaller, alpine form, *Viola adunca* var. *bellidifolia,* is 1/2 to 2″ high and grows Subalpine-Alpine. Colo. north.
2. **NORTHERN BOG VIOLET**—Flowers are violet color; paler at base with purple veins. The spur is thick and baggy and is 1/4 as long as the petals. Leaves are heart- or kidney-shaped; often purplish on the back. Has no plant stem so all leaves and flowers rise from the root crown. This violet is common in spring, in bogs and meadows of the lower zones. *Viola nephrophylla.*
3. **BIRDFOOT VIOLET**—is an early spring flower; violet-purple. Has no plant stem. Its leaves are divided into many narrow parts. Plains-Foothills. Southern Rockies. *Viola pedatifida.*

BLUE/SAUCER

131

PARRY HAREBELL
or Purple Bellflower
(p. 134)

5 petals. 7/8″ purplish-blue star flower <u>usually single,</u> and <u>facing up</u>. Creamy, 3-lobed pistil. Few narrow, alternate leaves.*

The delicate blue or violet petals have pointed tips. <u>Tiny white hairs grow *along the margins of the base of the lower stem leaves.</u> The single, erect, slender stem, 4-12″ tall, prefers moist meadows and the edge of aspen groves. Montane-Subalpine. *Campanula parryi,* Bellflower Family. Wyo. and Utah south.

MOUTAIN PHLOX
or ALPINE PHLOX
(See White/Saucer)

5 pale blue or lavender petals. 1/2″ flat flowers. Stamens are inside a slender 1/2″ tube with tiny opening at top. Needlelike leaves in loose mat or cushion 1-4″ high.

STORKSBILL
(See Red/Saucer)

5 petals. 3/8″ delicate flower. <u>Fernlike leaves,</u> often flat on ground. Bird-bill pods may turn upward. Plant 1-10″.

BLUE MUSTARD
or Spring Purpleweed
(p. 134)

4 "clawed" <u>petals widely separated.</u> Small, flat flower. Leaves alternate, toothed, often with leaf-like stipules at the axils. Stout stems 2-18″.

Flowers may be blue or lavender or bluish-purple. A "clawed" petal is very narrow at base. Lower leaves resemble small dandelion leaves but wither early. Plant often grows in large patches, turning whole fields to blue or pinkish-lavender. Apr-Jun. Plains-Foothills. Naturalized from Asia. *Chorispora tenella,* Mustard Family.

BLUE-EYED-GRASS
(p. 134)

<u>6 pointed lobes.</u> 1/2″ star flower with purple lines. Base of petals yellow. <u>Grass-like plant.</u> Damp meadows.

Bright blue to purple flower blooms only in bright sunshine. The 3 petals and 3 sepals are all alike. Because of the resemblance, this plant is called Blue-eyed-grass but it is not a grass at all; it is related to iris. Grows on damp slopes and meadows. Plains-Subalpine. *Sisyrinchium montanum,* Iris Family.

BLUE/SAUCER

ALPINE FORGET-ME-NOT (p. 134)	5 petals. 1/4″ sky-blue flowers with bright, <u>yellow-eye centers</u>. Soft white hairs on leaves. Gray cushion plant 1-3″ high. Alpine.

The brilliant blue flowers (rarely white) are delicately fragrant. They frequently bloom in a small dense mass. Tiny leaves, in silvery rosettes, form a cushion in rocky places, often near the top of high peaks. *Eritrichium elongatum, or argenteum,* Borage Family.

MOSS GENTIAN	5 (or 4) petals. Single 1/3″ star flower that <u>closes if shaded in any way.</u> Plant 1/2 to 4″. Chiefly alpine. Plaited gentian.*

*A plaited gentian has tiny, toothed folds of tissue between the petals (same color). Colo. north. *Gentiana prostrata,* Gentian Family.

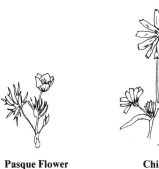

Pasque Flower   Chicory   Blue Lettuce

Wild Blue Flax

Spiderwort

Mountain Blue Violet

Birdfoot Violet

Parry Harebell

Blue Mustard

Blue-eyed Grass

Alpine Forget-me-not

COLORADO COLUMBINE
(p. 138)
(color plate p. 106)

"Cup and saucer" flower 2-3″ wide. White cup or bowl of 5 rounded, widely separated petals; and a blue saucer of 5 pointed sepals. Also, 5 long slender spurs. 3 leaflets.

This is the Colorado state flower. Digging or picking the columbine is prohibited by law in this state because, although abundant when Edwin James discovered it over 160 years ago near Palmer Lake, it has now become so scarce that without protection it would soon be extinct.

The white petals form a shallow cup and their bases extend backwards between the sepals to form hollow, blue-lavender spurs 1-2″ long. Lavender to rich blue or purple sepals form a star-shaped saucer for the white cup. In the center are many 1/2″ yellow-tipped stamens. The leaves, mostly basal on long stalks, are divided into 3 delicate, thin leaflets with rounded lobes; are rather lacy in appearance. Plant frequently has several stems 1-2′ high, and it grows in moist, shady places. Colorado Columbine is found throughout the U.S. Rockies, but west and north of Colorado, and at high altitudes, the deep blue color is often replaced by pale blue or white. Foothills-Alpine. *Aquilegia caerulea,* Buttercup Family.

NOTES. The name, columbine, comes from "columbia", meaning dove, from a fancied resemblance of the inverted flower to 5 doves.

Once in a while a columbine flower without any spurs may be found.

DWARF COLUMBINE—is a miniature species infrequently found among rocks at high altitudes. Its small, drooping flowers have short, curved or hooked spurs. Apparently limited to Colorado. *Aquilegia saximontana.*

WILD IRIS
or Blue Flag,
or Rocky Mtn. Iris
(p. 138)

Large flower with 3 big drooping, veined sepals; 3 erect petals; and 3 wide, erect, petal-like pistils. Sword-like leaves.

Color varies from pale blue to violet, and the flower is borne on a leafless stalk. A stamen stands between each sepal and pistil. The common base of the flowers and buds is enclosed in a wide sheath. There are several long, flat, slender, pointed leaves. The sturdy stem, 8-24″ tall, resembles the cultivated iris. Although sometimes found on dry ground, it prefers wet meadows where it often grows in large colonies. Foothills-Subalpine. *Iris missouriensis,* Iris Family.

NOTES. The iris (fleur de lis) was the royal emblem of France. The name, iris, is from the Greek word for "rainbow", referring to the many colors of different varieties. (The Rocky Mountain region has only one species—this blue one.)

Iris roots have a strong, disagreeable odor and they contain the poison, irisin, which is used in medicine. American Indians ground the roots of iris and prepared a poison for their arrow points.

Iris has no forage value. The orris root of commerce comes from the fragrant root of one species. The roasted seeds of some species have been used in Great Britain as a coffee substitute.

CLEMATIS	4 slender "petals"—often widely
(p. 138)	separated. 1-1/2" flower, pale blue to lavender-purple, droops on a long stalk. Leaves opposite, divided in 3's once or twice. Plant is a vine. 2 species follow:

1. **COLUMBIA CLEMATIS or BLUE CLEMATIS**—The veined sepals look just like petals (clematis has no true petals.) They are veined, pointed, and widely spread out. There are 3 large leaflets, entire or toothed. This slender, trailing, semi-woody vine is 10-12' long and grows in moist, shady woods. In autumn, the silky-plumed seed clusters are conspicuous. Foothills-Subalpine. *Clematis columbiana*, Buttercup Family.

2. **ROCKY MOUNTAIN CLEMATIS or SUBALPINE CLEMATIS**—like the preceding but:
   A. The sepals may spread or they may be nearly closed like a tiny lantern.
   B. The 3 leaflets are each divided into 3 smaller leaflets that are toothed or lobed.
   C. Vine is more delicate and is seldom over 5' long. *Clematis pseudoalpina*.

SUGAR-BOWL	One drooping, urn-shaped flower
or Vase Flower	1-1/2" long, and deep purple inside,
or Leather Flower	hangs from each erect stem. "Petal"
(p. 138)	tips turn back. Leaves opposite, gray-
(color plate p. 107)	hairy and have 5 to 13 leaflets.

Flower is shaped like an urn or a sugar bowl upside down. The inside is purple but the outside looks paler because it is so hairy. Flower has no true petals but the thick, leathery sepals look just like petals. Later on, the flowers develop silky, feathery seed plumes. Leaves variable but are usually finely divided. Plant is hairy, bushy, 1-2' tall, and grows on open slopes. Foothills-Montane. *Clematis hirsutissima*, Buttercup Family.

HAREBELL or Scotch Bluebell *(p. 138)* *(color plate p. 106)*	5 pointed petals. Usually several drooping 3/4″ bell flowers. Leaves alternate, linear. Slender, wiry stem, 6-18″.

There are generally 3 or more lavender to violet-blue flowers on a stem, and they hang with a slight tilt. Basal leaves (if any, because they wither early) are small and rounded; stem leaves are 1-3″ long. Flower is widespread in various kinds of locations. At high altitudes, the stem may be only 2″ or 3″ tall but the bells are just as large. May-Oct. *Campanula rotundifolia,* Bellflower Family.

NOTES. Harebells grow in northern countries, including Scotland, and are the "Bluebells" famous in Scottish songs and stories.

Harebells might be confused with Parry Harebells but: Harebell—flower is bell-shaped; usually nodding; usually several flowers. Parry H.—flower is funnel-form; always erect; usually one flower.

Harebell—has sepals about 1/4″ long. Parry H.—sepals usually 1/2″ long; and lower leaf bases and petioles are edged with little, white hairs.

MAT PENSTEMON *(p. 138)*	2-lipped flowers (see Key Terms) 5/8″ long. Blue to purplish. Tiny leaves. Plant forms a mat under 3″ in height (or 4-6″).*

Lower lip extends out beyond the upper one. Leaves, less than 1″ long, may be grayish or green. Plant forms a thin, compact 3″ mat sometimes up to 4′ in diam. It may be densely covered with flowers. Occurs in western Wyo., N.W. Colo. and N.E. Utah on clay or rocky soil in sagebrush country. Foothills-Montane. *Penstemon caespitosus,* Figwort Family.

*CRANDALL PENSTEMON—is similar but it forms a thick mat 4-6″ high of small green leaves, each tipped with a tiny blunt tooth. In loamy soil; Montane zone from central Colo. south and west into Utah. *Penstemon crandallii.*

LARGE-BRACTED VERBENA or Vervain *(p. 138)*	5 petals. Small flat clusters of tiny blue to purple flowers with long, conspicuous bracts. Leaves opposite, lobed along sides; rough. Stems usually prostrate.

Narrow, stiff, hairy bracts extend beyond the flowers, sometimes partially concealing them. Many small leaves. Much branched

137

plant with rough, hairy branches spreading along the ground. The stem ends, however, often turn up. In gardens, fields, and along roads. Plains-Foothills. *Verbena bracteata,* Vervain Family.

NOTE. This little verbena is closely related to the cultivated verbenas, and all are related to the teak tree of East India which may be over 100' tall. Teak wood is extremely valuable because it is highly resistant to insects and to warping. It is used for fine flooring and furniture and was once used in ship-building. Its leaves furnish a red dye.

| **BLUE-EYED MARY** | 1/8", 2-lipped flower; blue, or blue and white. Leaves whorled or opposite and often purplish. Tiny plant usually under 2". |
| *(p. 138)* | |

Because of its diminutive size, this flower is often overlooked, although it is very common. There may be 1 to 5 flowers. Stem is 1-2" high (rarely to 12"). Foothills-Montane. Apr-Jul. *Collinsia parviflora,* Figwort Family.

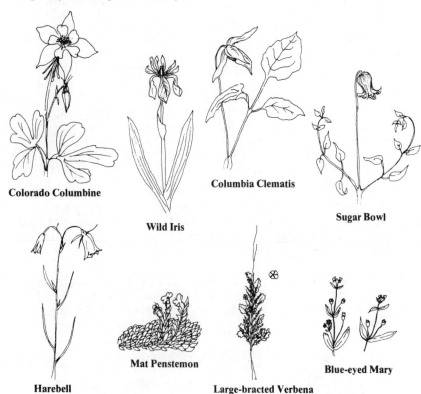

Colorado Columbine

Wild Iris

Columbia Clematis

Sugar Bowl

Harebell

Mat Penstemon

Large-bracted Verbena

Blue-eyed Mary

138

Fernleaf Lousewort
(p. 162)

Golden Banner
(p. 163)

Shrubby Cinquefoil
(p. 157)

Yellow Paintbrush
(p. 169)

139

Butter-and-eggs
(p. 161)

Black-eyed Susan
(p. 145)

Sunflower
(p. 143-144)

Gumweed
(p. 147)

Common Spring Senecio
(p. 151)

Parsley
(p. 171-172)

Yellow Stemless Evening-primrose
(p. 177)

Colo. Rubber Plant
(p. 149)

Wallflower
(p. 170)

Sawtoothed Senecio
(p. 152)

Snow Buttercup
(p. 181-182)

Woolly Actinea
(p. 148)

MULE-EARS
(p. 154)

3-5″ flower. Both center and rays yellow. Stem leaves alternate; basal leaves 8-16″ long and 2-6″ wide. They look varnished.*

There may be one flower or several in a cluster with the end one largest. Bracts are leaf-like. Leaves are glossy, sticky, and may be entire or toothed. The basal ones are leathery; stem leaves are smaller and clasping. Coarse plant, 1-2′ tall, has no hair. Found in moist soil. Montane-Subalpine. From northwest Colo. to Nev. and Mont. *Wyethia amplexicaulis,* Composite Family.

NOTE. It was named Wyethia for Capt. N.J. Wyeth, the man who established the first American fur trading post in the Northwest—Fort Hall near Pocatello, Idaho.

*ARIZONA MULE-EARS—similar to the preceding but the plant is very hairy—not glossy. Found from Colo. and Utah south. Foothills-Montane. There are hybrids between the two species. *Wyethia arizonica.*

TALL CONEFLOWER
or Golden Glow
(p. 154)

2-5″ flower. Drooping rays. Yellowish, egg-shaped cone 1″ high. Leaves alternate, with large, toothed lobes. Plant 2-6′ tall. Along creeks.

The yellow rays, 1 to 2-1/2″ long, usually have 2 blunt teeth at the end. Center cone is greenish-yellow or brownish-yellow. Leaves, up to 5″ wide, are smooth and deeply divided. Plant has one to several grooved, woody stems. Common along mountain creeks. Foothills-Montane. *Rudbeckia laciniata* var. *ampla,* Composite Family.

KANSAS SUNFLOWER
(p. 154)
(color plate p. 140)

2-5″ flower, yellow rays, dark center. Bracts have bristly-hairy fringe and long-pointed tips. Leaves mostly alternate; lower ones often heart-shaped. Very rough-hairy plant.

The dark-brown or dark reddish-purple center is flat or nearly so. This center is not always perfectly even because at one stage, the styles of the little disk flowers are raised slightly; at another stage, the anthers are elevated. The ray tips are toothed, and there may be several blossoms. The broad leaves are 2-10″ long. Plant usually has one branched stem 1-8′ tall and is very common along roadsides and in fields. Plains-Foothills. *Helianthus annuus,* Composite Family.

NOTES. This is the state flower of Kansas.
    Indians around Lake Huron were cultivating sunflowers when

French explorers first arrived. They used sunflower seeds as food, obtained oil from the seeds, fiber from the stems, and a yellow dye from the flowers. We now value the sunflower plant as good silage, we eat the seeds, use them as poultry feed, and make a high-grade oil from them for cooking and for use in paints.

Cultivated sunflowers may attain a height of 20 feet with flowers 1' wide.

PRAIRIE SUNFLOWER—looks just like Kansas Sunflower but the bracts are NOT bristly-hairy nor long-pointed; and the leaves are narrower. These two species often grow together and they hybridize freely. *Helianthus petiolaris.*

ASPEN SUNFLOWER or Little Sunflower	Looks like the preceding but center is yellow, and flower—usually single—faces sideways on bent stem. 4 (or 5) pairs of opposite, entire leaves; all are long, 5-nerved, smooth and glossy. In or near woods.

The center is deep yellow and the toothed rays are a lighter yellow. Flower may or may not be solitary. The leathery leaves have 5 main veins. Plant, 1-4' tall and unbranched, is closely related to the true sunflower but is found in damp, open woods and aspen groves. Montane-Subalpine. *Helianthella quinquenervis,* Composite Family.

BUSH SUNFLOWER *(p. 154)*	Many 2″ flowers, yellow rays, center brownish-yellow. Leaves mostly opposite. Bushy; several stiff stems, 1 to 2-1/2'. Plant very rough-hairy. Dry hillsides.

The numerous flower heads have bright rays but dingy or dull brownish-yellow, nearly flat centers. Abundant on open, sunny hillsides on the eastern slope in Wyo. and Colo. Plains-Foothills. *Helianthus pumilus,* Composite Family.

NOTE. This might be confused with Kansas Sunflower or Prairie S. but they both have dark centers, leaves mostly alternate, and usually one branched stem. The Bush Sunflower center is dull brownish-yellow, leaves are mostly opposite, and there are always several, stiff stems.

144

ALPINE GOLDFLOWER or Old-Man-of-the-Mountain or Alpine Sunflower or Sun God, or Mtn. Sunflower, or Rydbergia. Take your choice! *(p. 154)*	3″ flower facing east; <u>densely soft-woolly</u> at base of head, yellow center, bright rays toothed. Soft, gray-green leaves <u>cut into linear parts</u>. Alpine.

Flower, 2-4″ wide, has 20 to 50 flat, yellow rays which are wide at the outer end with 3 large teeth. In the center, are about 100 golden disk flowers. These are the largest blossoms above timberline—very conspicuous. If you see a number of them facing in one direction, you will know that way is east. Leaves are woolly, with loose, white hairs. The stout stems, 2-12″ tall, grow on rocky ridges, Colo. and Utah north. *Hymenoxys grandiflora* or *Rydbergia grandiflora,* Composite Family.

ARROWLEAF BALSAMROOT *(p. 154)*	3″ flower, yellow rays and center. Woolly bracts. Leaves <u>mostly basal</u> 8-15″ long, <u>entire</u>, <u>arrow-shaped</u>, and soft-grayish.

Usually one flower on an 8-24″ stalk. The pointed, overlapping bracts have soft, white hairs. The long-petioled leaves are velvety-hairy, with pointed tips but the 2 lobes which extend downwards are rounded. A few small stem leaves. Plant is coarse and very leafy; it grows on dry, open, sunny slopes west of the Continental Divide. Foothills-Montane. *Balsamorhiza sagittata,* Composite Family.

BLACK-EYED SUSAN or Brown-eyed Susan *(p. 154)* *(color plate p. 140)*	3″ flower; yellowish rays, blackish cone 1/4 to 1/2″ high. All leaves alternate, lance-shaped, entire. Hairy plant. Stem may be purple-dotted. Often in aspen groves.

Usually one sunflower-like blossom on each stem. Pointed, grooved rays. The center is a smooth black or dark-brown cone, usually wider than it is high. A few fringy-hairy disk flowers may surround the cone base. Leaves, 1-4″ long, have a strong midrib. Plant is 1-2′ tall and grows in meadows and aspen groves. Foothills-Montane. The stem is usually closely sprinkled with purple dots. *Rudbeckia hirta,* Composite Family.

NOTE. Black-eyed Susan might be confused with Prairie Sunflower but:

SUSAN

Often has purple dots on stem. Is hairy but not especially rough. Usually in meadows and aspen groves. Rays are yellow; may tend towards orange.

P. SUNFLOWER

Never any dots on stem. Is definitely rough-hairy. More common in hot, dry places. Rays are bright yellow.

GAILLARDIA
or Blanketflower
(p. 154)

2-1/2" flower. Deeply slit, wide, flat rays. Red, cone-like center. Hairy, rough plant, 8-20". Leaves alternate.

Wide, dark red center and bright orange or yellow rays that are slit for 1/3 or more of their length. Stiff, silvery hairs cover base of flower head. Leaves, 2-8" long, have a white midrib and may be entire or toothed or lobed. Plant usually has several erect stems, and grows on dry hills and meadows. Foothills-Timberline. *Gaillardia aristata,* Composite Family.

NOTE. Gaillardia has been cultivated and is now grown in flower gardens over a large part of the world.

CURLYHEAD
  GOLDENWEED
(p. 154)

3" flower; yellow center, orange-yellow, strap-shaped rays that tend to curl backwards. All leaves alternate and petioled; upper ones much smaller. Several 10-24" stems.

Flowers are usually solitary on a stem, with several rows of overlapping bracts. The rays curl backward as the flower ages. Plant has stout stems and grows on the western slope from Wyo. and Utah south. Montane-Subalpine. *Haplopappus croceus,* Composite Family.

ARNICA
(p. 155)

Usually 1 to 3 flowers, each 1-3" wide; look like a sunflower but center is yellow. Leaves opposite and green. Grows mainly in meadows and forests. 5 common species follow.

In the composite family (Daisy type) each tiny style—top of the pistil—is usually branched, supporting 2 stigmas which generally curl under gracefully. In arnica flowers, these 2-headed pistils give a porous or honeycomb effect more noticeable than in the center of other composites.

1. **HEART-LEAF ARNICA**—The 9 to 13 toothed rays are widely separated at the tips. Just below the flower head are long, white hairs. Pappus is white. (If the pappus interests you, see Glossary and the diagram of a Composite Flower in back of book.) There are 2 or 3 pairs of leaves. The <u>lower ones are heart-shaped</u> with <u>petioles as long as the blades.</u> Usually a single, bright blossom tops a single, hairy stem 8-18″ tall; growing, often in clumps, in moist, shady locations in conifer forests. Montane-Subalpine. *Arnica cordifolia,* Composite Family.

   NOTE. Heart-leaf is the showiest of all arnicas. The dried flowers of another species, Arnica montana, furnish the tincture used on bruises and sprains.

2. **BROAD-LEAF ARNICA**—very similar to Heart-leaf Arnica but has no white hairs below flower head; and it may have 1 to 5 flowers on a stem. Occurs throughout the Rockies. *Arnica latifolia.*

3. **MEADOW ARNICA or ORANGE ARNICA**—There are 12 to 20 orange-yellow, toothed rays. Usually one flower head; sometimes 2 or 3. Pappus is brownish or yellowish. Leaves, 2 or 3 pairs, are narrow and sticky-hairy; lower ones have <u>petioles shorter than the blades.</u> Plant is strongly scented and grows in meadows. Foothills-Montane. Colo. to Canada. There are <u>tufts of brownish hair in the axils of leaves at base of plant.</u> *Arnica fulgens.*

4. **SUBALPINE ARNICA**—Flowers have 14 to 18 rays; the pappus is yellowish-brown; there are 3 to 4 pairs of leaves; and plant is 8-20″ tall. Subalpine-Alpine. Colo. to Canada. *Arnica mollis. (p. 155)*

5. **ALPINE ARNICA**—Flowers, about 1″ wide, have white pappus. 3 pairs of leaves. Plant grows on rocky slopes at and above timberline. Colo. to Canada. It is 4-10″ tall and has 4 to 10 rays. *Arnica rydbergii.*

GUMWEED *(p. 155)* *(color plate p. 140)*	1-1/4″ flowers; yellow centers and rays. <u>Very sticky flowers and buds, with down-curved bracts.</u> Stiff leaves, toothed.

The fragrant flowers have a very sticky 1/2″ involucre of narrow bracts that curve down. The round buds, too, are sticky and white-gummy, with bracts curling down. Leaves are alternate, clasping, and thick. Plant is 8-30″ tall, coarse, woody and much-branched near top. Very common along roads and in disturbed soil. Plains-

147

Subalpine. Wyo. to Ariz. and Tex. *Grindelia squarrosa* and *Grindelia subalpina,* Composite Family.

NOTE. Gumweed is used in medicine, including treatment for poison ivy cases. Indians used it as medicine, and also steeped the leaves for tea.

GOLDENEYE or Sunspots *(p. 155)*	Many 1-1/4″ flowers; rays yellow, centers yellow to brown. Ray tips often turn white when aging. Lower leaves opposite. Erect, 1-3′ stem. Much branched.

Like small sunflowers but have yellow to brownish center cone perhaps 1/4″ high. Usually 9 to 12 bright rays. No pappus. 1-3″ leaves are linear to lance-shaped, entire or toothed and somewhat rough. Plant has one or more stems, and is very common in late summer. Foothills-Montane. *Gymnolomia* or *Viguiera multiflora,* Composite Family.

NOTE. This might be confused with Bush Sunflower, but the latter has several stiff, sturdy stems, is very rough-hairy, and blooms Jun-Aug. Goldeneye has slender stems branched at top, is somewhat rough, and blooms Aug-Sep.

ACTINEA *(p. 155)*	3/4″ flower, yellow center; rays toothed and veined. Leaves all basal* narrow, entire, usually silvery-hairy. Plant 2-15″.

Flowers may be single or in a loose cluster. The strap-shaped rays have orange veins. Leaves, 1-2″ long, are rather stiff. Sometimes there is one *small leaf on the stem. Plant starts blooming early in spring on very short stalks that may be either silvery-hairy or green; grows in dry places. Foothills *Hymenoxys,* or *Actinea acaulis,* Composite Family.

WOOLLY ACTINEA *(p. 155)* *(color plate p. 142)*	1-1/4″ flower; yellow center, toothed rays. Back of flower head very woolly. Leaves uncut and usually woolly. Plant 1-2″ high. Alpine.

This is an alpine variety of the preceding. The woolly flower head nestles close to the ground among the—usually—silvery-woolly leaves. Plant grows in exposed rocky places. Wyo. and Utah south. *Hymenoxys,* or *Actinea acaulis* var. *caespitosa.*

COLORADO RUBBER PLANT
(p. 155)
(color plate p. 141)

Flat clusters of 3/4″ yellow flowers; rays wide at outer end with 3 teeth.* Leaves alternate, divided, thread-like but firm. Woolly hairs in leaf axils. Woody stems. Some basal leaves.

The many heads have yellow centers, and each flower has 8 (rarely to 14) *yellow rays which are flat at first but in aging, they all droop and form a little flaring skirt around the bowl-shaped flower base. Both basal and stem leaves are numerous, and 1-1/2 to 4″ long. They are divided into 3 to 7 linear, fleshy parts. The several woody stems, 4-18″ tall, are much branched at top. Some withered growth often surrounds the base of the plant. It grows in sunny, dry, rocky places. Foothills-Montane. Despite the name, it is found throughout the U.S. Rockies. *Hymenoxys richardsonii,* Composite Family.

NOTE. As the name suggests, this plant contains some rubber.

GOLDEN-ASTER
or Goldeneye
(p. 155)

Numerous 3/4″ flowers; yellow centers, 12 to 25 yellow rays. Bracts are overlapping. Flowers are at ends of low stems.* Narrow, alternate, entire, gray-green leaves, hairy and often rough.

Flowers have narrow rays and look like small, scrawny asters but they are not asters. One or more flowers tip each of the usually spreading stems. *The numerous woody stems 4-18″ long, may be erect but generally they spread out, gradually rising towards the tips.
This variable, hardy, wide-spread plant is hairy and may be rough. It often appears thin and dried out. Plains-Subalpine. *Heterotheca, or Chrysopsis villosa,* Composite Family.

PRAIRIE CONEFLOWER

Cylindrical cone 1/2 to 1-1/2″ long (or more), on long stalk. 3 to 7 wide yellow rays at base of cone. Leaves much cut. Plant 1 to 2-1/2′. Dry plains.

Cone usually brownish-purple. Rays yellow—or purplish. They sometimes droop. Leaves alternate, divided into oblong or linear parts. Branched plant, on hills and valleys. Plains-Foothills. *Ratibida columnifera,* Composite Family.

149

CALTHA-FLOWERED BUTTERCUP (See Yellow/Saucers)	1/2 to 1″ <u>waxy flower</u>, 5 to 10 oblong petals. Many stamens. <u>All leaves un-divided,</u> long, pointed, entire. Plant erect.

This Saucer flower might be confused with the Daisy Group (Composites) because its stamens and pistils are so closely packed in the center. But composite flowers never look waxy or varnished.

WILD CHRYSANTHEMUM *(p. 155)*	Clusters of 1″ flowers; <u>short wide rays</u>, large, yellow center. <u>Leaves much-cut</u>, gray-green; <u>in basal rosette</u> and <u>alternate; smaller</u> on the single, erect, 1-3′ stem.

Flowers have 12 to 18 broad, yellow rays that are shorter than the width of the flower center. Leaves are 2 or 3 times divided into oblong or linear parts. Plant is branched at top. It grows in gravelly soil from Wyo. to Mexico. Foothills-Montane. *Bahia dissecta,* Composite Family.

ALPINE GOLDENWEED or Alpine Tonestus *(p. 156)*	3/4″ bright flower. Yellow rays and center. Bracts <u>leaf-like, loose, overlapping, look disordered.</u> Leaves alternate and/or basal. Dwarf plants 1-6″ high. Alpine only.

Flower solitary on stem with bracts tapering to sharp point. Leaves alternate and erect; wider near tip, usually entire. Leafy stems <u>2-6″ high</u>. From Colo. north and west. *Haplopappus* or *Tonestus lyallii,* Composite Family.
PYGMY GOLDENWEED or PYGMY TONESTUS—similar to the above but bracts may be pointed or blunt; the few, narrow leaves are mostly basal; and the several to many stems form a <u>little cushion 1-2″ high</u>. Wyo. to New Mex. *Haplopappus pygmaeus.*

SENECIO or Groundsel or Ragwort or Butterweed	Flowers, 1/4 to 1-1/2″ wide, have yellow centers and rays; and the rays are usually <u>widely separated</u>. Flowers are usually in loose clusters. Bracts, narrow and equal are in <u>1 smooth, neat row,</u> although sometimes there may be a few short or straggly bracts at the base. The bracts may or may not be black-tipped. Leaves are <u>always alternate</u>. On the following pages are 10 senecios.

The name, Senecio, comes from a Latin word meaning "old man", referring to the white pappus which looks like white hair when the senecios go to seed.

The Senecios are a large group with more than 40 species in the state of Colorado. The flowers of most face up but a few are nodding (turned sideways or downward.) The plants may be smooth—without hair—or may be cobwebby with soft, white hairs, but are never rough with stiff hairs, like sunflowers.

The senecios in this region all have yellow rays with one exception, the SAFFRON SENECIO *Senecio crocatus,* which has orange or orange-red rays and two kinds of leaves: basal ones entire or toothed; stem leaves lobed.

All senecios, of course, belong to the Composite Family.

COMMON SPRING SENECIO or Lambstongue Groundsel *(p. 156)* *(color plate p. 141)*	Uneven cluster of 3/4″ flowers; central flower usually on shortest stalk. Few rays, Upper leaves smaller and tapered. Erect plant, 8-24″; may be hairy. Variable. Stout stem. Apr -Aug.

Narrow, irregular rays. The central flower is generally larger. Bracts may be black-tipped. Leaves, usually entire, point upwards, upper ones often clasp, and they taper to a slender point. In spring the whole plant is semi-woolly and yellowish-green with loose, white hairs. Later on, these hairs disappear. Foothills-Subalpine. Colo. to Canada. *Senecio integerrimus.*

DAFFODIL SENECIO *(p. 156)*	1″ nodding flower. Buds also nod. Light yellow rays, slightly darker center. Bracts sometimes purplish. Leaves quite firm.

Leaves, 2-6″ long, may be toothed or entire; are usually sessile, may clasp the stem. The leafy stems are commonly 6-12″. Plant grows in rocky timberline regions in Colo. and Wyo. west to Nev. *Senecio amplectens.*

ROCK RAGWORT or Rock Senecio *(p. 156)*	Clusters of 1-1/2″ flowers; bright yellow centers and rays. Leaves are thick-textured, coarsely toothed, alternate, ovate. Bushy. Stems 4-20″, spreading at base.

Few to several flower heads on each stem; 8 to 16 rays. Plant has stout, leafy, light green stems, and grows on road banks and rocky slides. Subalpine-Alpine. This or a very similar species is found from New Mex. to Montana. *Senecio fremontii* var. *blitoides,* or *carthamoides.*

TRIANGLE-LEAF S. or Triangle-leaf Ragwort, or Arrowleaf Senecio, or Butterweed *(p. 156)* *(color plate p. 142)*	Clusters of 1″ flowers; yellow center, 6 or 8 widely separated rays. Long, alternate, toothed, <u>triangular leaves,</u> <u>widest near the base.</u> Plant 2-5′. <u>In</u> <u>wet places.</u>

Many loose flower clusters over top of plant. Leaves, 2-6″ long, have <u>teeth pointing outward</u>. Plant is one of the tallest senecios. It is unbranched and grows in tall, leafy clumps in wet ground. Subalpine. The young shoots are poisonous. *Senecio triangularis.*

TOOTHED SENECIO or **SAWTOOTHED BUTTER-WEED**—very similar to the preceding but its leaves are lance-shaped to linear, <u>and are widest in the middle,</u> with narrower base and long-pointed tips; <u>sharp teeth directed</u> forward. Montane-Subalpine. Colo. to Montana. *Senecio serra,* var. *admirabilis. (p. 156)*

WOOTON SENECIO *(p. 156)*	3/4″ flowers; 8 to 10 bright rays and yellow center. Leaves are alternate and mostly basal, <u>spoon-shaped, and</u> <u>bluish-green like cabbage.</u> <u>Not hairy.</u> <u>Winged petioles.</u>

Leaves are thick-textured, and of an unusual bluish-green color. The petioles broaden at base into wings. Plant has several 6-20″ stems, and grows on moist gravel slopes in Colo. and New Mex. Subalpine-Alpine. *Senecio wootonii.* It was named for the botanist, W. W. Wooton.

BLACK-TIPPED **SENECIO** *(p. 156)*	Uneven clusters of 1/2″ flowers; yellowish centers, <u>3 to 5 widely</u> <u>separated rays.</u> Bracts have conspicuous <u>black tips.</u> Soft, silvery-gray to <u>whitish leaves 1-2″ wide.</u> Stout, silvery stem 8-30″.

Numerous flower clusters 1-5″ wide. Leaves are basal and alternate; oblong to spoon-shaped, entire or toothed, at least 1″ wide and several inches long, and soft-woolly. Found almost exclusively in the subalpine zone, growing—often in large clumps—on slopes and along roads in Colo. Utah, and New Mex. *Senecio atratus.*

FENDLER SENECIO
or Fendler Groundsel
(p. 156)

Loose cluster of flowers; 7 to 12 rays. Narrow, alternate, grayish leaves, often folded; have even, coarse, comb-like lobes on each side. Plant generally under 12″, unbranched.

Yellow rays and centers. Leaf lobes may be short or deeply cut like the teeth of a comb. Plant, when young, is gray with soft, silvery, matted hairs. Later, the hairs disappear and the plant becomes green and smooth. Branched only in the flower cluster. Common in gravelly soils, Wyo. to New Mex. Foothills-Subalpine. *Senecio fendleri.*

WESTERN GOLDEN RAGWORT
(p. 156)

Clusters of 1/2″ flowers; yellow rays and centers. Leaves alternate; deeply, pinnately divided into unequal, toothed parts. Bushy plants 1-2′ tall; leafy-stemmed.

Flowers bloom profusely, often covering plant. Leaves are 1-4″ long and dark green; all about the same size. Plant is common along roads and on gravelly slopes. Montane-Subalpine. Ida. and Wyo. to Ariz. and New Mex. *Senecio eremophilus.*

BROOM SENECIO
or Grass-leaf Senecio
(p. 156)

Loose clusters of 1/4″ flowers; yellowish centers, usually 5 narrow, sulphur-yellow rays, very widely separated. Bracts form an even 1/2″ cylinder. Many alternate, green, linear leaves, entire or with linear lobes. Bushy plant.

This 8-24″ plant is non-hairy, very leafy, and intricately branched. It is common along roadsides, well covered with yellow flowers. Plains-Montane. Jul-Sep. Wyo. and Nebr. to Ariz. and Tex. *Senecio spartioides.*

Mule-ears

Tall Coneflower

Kansas Sunflower

Bush Sunflower

Alpine Goldflower

Arrowleaf Balsamroot

Black-eyed Susan

Gaillardia

Curlyhead Goldenweed

154

Heart-leaf Arnica

Subalpine Arnica

Gumweed

Goldeneye

Actinea

Woolly Actinea

Colorado Rubber Plant

Golden Aster

Wild Chrysanthemum

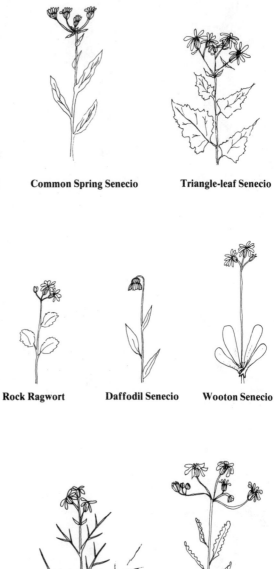

Pigmy Goldenweed   **Common Spring Senecio**   **Triangle-leaf Senecio**

**Western Golden
Ragwort**   **Rock Ragwort**   **Daffodil Senecio**   **Wooton Senecio**

Black· ..ped Senecio   **Broom Senecio**   **Fendler Senecio**

156

SHRUBBY
  CINQUEFOIL
or Bush Cinquefoil
(p. 160)
(color plate p. 139)

> 5 wide, rounded petals. 1″ bright saucer flowers. Many stamens. Usually 5 narrow, entire leaflets. Dense, gray-green shrub.

Leaves are alternate and have 3 to 7 leathery leaflets, 3/4″ long. This rounded shrub, varying in size from several inches in the alpine zone to 3 or 4′ in lower altitudes, is actually a thornless yellow rose which blooms continuously May-Sep. The branching stems have dark, shreddy bark. Shrub likes moist ground and is widespread in northern regions of the world. *Potentilla fruticosa,* or *Dasiphora fruticosa,* Rose Family.

NOTES. Shrubby Cinquefoil is an "indicator" plant that shows the condition of the range. Neither livestock nor big game will eat it unless other food is scarce. Consequently when stock owners or wildlife biologists find Shrubby Cinquefoil overgrazed, they know that there are more livestock or big game on the range than it can support.

About 30 species of cinquefoil (SINK foil) grow in this area. All except Shrubby Cinquefoil are herbs, i.e., plants whose stems die back to the ground each autumn.

The generic name, potentilla, comes from the Latin potens, meaning powerful, referring to the former use of potentilla in medicine. The common name, cinquefoil, is from a French word meaning "5-finger", and was originally applied to a European species with 5 leaflets.

GOLDEN CURRANT
or Buffalo Currant
or Clove Bush
(p. 160)

> 5 short, spreading petals, separated. Loose clusters of golden tube flowers 1/2″ long. Red stamens, greenish pistil. Leaves have 3 lobes—rarely 5.

Flowers bloom Apr-Jun, have a spicy fragrance, and are often tinged with red. Leaves are smooth, often in clusters, and in autumn, they turn red or rose. The 2 to 9′ shrub is found along watercourses or in open places. Plains-Foothills. Fruit is edible; may be black or red. *Ribes aureum.* Gooseberry Family.

TWINBERRY
  HONEYSUCKLE
or Swamp Honeysuckle
(p. 160)

> Pairs of tube flowers 1/2″ long with leafy bracts; on short stems. Later, black fruit in red bracts. Leaves opposite, large, entire.

The yellow flowers are always in pairs and are surrounded by bracts that turn red or purplish-red as the twin fruits ripen to a shiny black. Pointed leaves are 2-6″ long. Shrub, 2-9′ tall, is quite leafy, and grows in rich moist soil, often along streams. Foothills-Subalpine. It is visited by humming birds. *Lonicera involucrata,* Honeysuckle Family.

ANTELOPE-BRUSH or Bitterbrush *(p. 160)*	5 <u>pale petals</u>. 1/2″ fragrant saucer flowers. Clusters of 1″ <u>wedge-shaped leaves</u> with 3 large teeth at end. Low dense shrub near rocks.

Although they occur singly, the flowers are sometimes so dense that the shrub is almost entirely covered with little, pale yellow blossoms. The petals are widely separated with light green sepals visible between. Leaves, 1/3 to 1″ long, are green above and whitish below; are fairly thick in alternate clusters. In very dry weather, they may turn yellow. Shrub is 2-4′ tall (rarely 10′) and is intricately branched. It grows on dry slopes, often near rocks. Foothills-Montane. The small pods are extremely bitter. *Purshia tridentata,* Rose Family.

NOTE. Antelope brush is usually seen as a low shrub because it is a favorite browse for both wild game and livestock. Small rodents eat large quantities of the seeds.

SMOOTH SUMAC (See Other Colors/Shrub)	3/8″ pale flowers in <u>long pointed heads</u>. 5 petals. Alternate leaves with 12 to 21 narrow, toothed leaflets, green above, pale below. Sandy banks and along roads.

THREE-LEAF SUMAC or Skunkbush *(p. 160)*	Tight clusters of 1/8″ pale <u>flowers bloom before leaves open</u>. Leaves have 3 wedge-shaped leaflets at tip of petiole. Dense shrub.

Tiny yellowish petals and an orange center. Buds are yellow-green. Leaflets are 1/4 to 1-1/4″; <u>middle one is largest</u>. All are dark green above and paler below. Leaves often in clusters. Shrub is 1-6′ tall and much branched. The red berries are sticky; may collect cobwebs and dust. Shrub is widespread. Plains-Montane. *Rhus trilobata,* Sumac Family.

NOTES. Because the wood is strong-smelling, it has been called Skunkbush.

    Indian women used the long, red shoots in weaving baskets.

    The berries can be made into a lemonade-like drink.

RABBIT-BRUSH
(p. 160)

Small heads of tiny disk flowers form golden masses. No rays nor petals. Linear, gray-green leaves. Shrub has many pale, woody twigs.

4 to 7 little tubular disk flowers are gathered in a head 1/4″ wide and 1/2″ long, with the base wrapped in green bracts. These heads form round-topped clusters sometimes so numerous that the entire top of the shrub becomes a golden mass. Leaves, 1-3″ long, are alternate, and fairly thick along stem. Shrub, 8″ to 6′ tall, is odorous, and variable. Its woody stems and branches are whitish or light green because they are covered with closely matted, white-woolly hair. If the bark is bruised, it has a fruity smell slightly like apples. Although it may grow near irrigated places, this is a typical desert shrub, able to thrive where many other plants cannot. Plains-Montane. Aug.-Oct. This rabbit-brush contains 2% to 6% rubber. *Chrysothamnus nauseosus,* Composite Family.

STICKY-FLOWERED RABBIT-BRUSH—like the preceding but it is shorter—10-24″ tall; has smaller flowers; its narrow leaves are usually twisted; and the twigs are green (have no hairs or very fine hairs.) Common on dry plains and hills west of the Continental Divide. *Chrysothamnus viscidiflorus* or *pumilus.*

NOTES. Although not relished by animals, the rabbit-brushes serve as a reserve food for jackrabbits, antelopes, mountain sheep and deer; in winter they are browsed by elk.

Indians made a yellow dye from the flowers, and used the stems as medicine and for thatching roofs.

Three-leaf Sumac

Shrubby Cinquefoil

Golden Currant

Twinberry Honeysuckle

Antelope-brush

Rabbitbrush

COMMON EVENING-PRIMROSE and **HOOKER** EVENING-PRIMROSE *(p. 166)*	4 wide, round petals. 1/2 to 2″ saucer flower. Long stamens; long stigma with 4 lobes. Sepals turn down. Leaves alternate, lance-shaped. Stem 6″-4′.

The bright yellow flowers open in the evening and close the next day when the sun gets hot. They turn to orange or red as they fade. The 4 sepal tips turn back down loosely instead of resting close to the petals. Leaves are toothed. The sturdy stem is hairy and stiffly erect; common along roadsides. Plains-Foothills. *Oenothera strigosa* and *O. hookeri,* Evening-Primrose Family. The strigosa flowers are less than 1″ wide; hookeri flowers are 1-2″.

NOTE. Evening-Primroses have an unusual calyx. Although it looks like a stem, it is actually a tube 1-6″ long, enclosing the style which leads from the 4-lobed stigma to the ovary. The stigma receives pollen, the style conducts this pollen down to the ovary and after the petals fall the ovary develops into the seed pod.

In the above species, the rather large ovary is situated in the leaf axil, where it becomes quite prominent.

BUTTER-AND-EGGS or Toadflax *(p. 166)* *(color plate p. 140)*	1″, 2-lipped flowers (see Key Terms) each with an orange spot and a long yellow spur pointing downwards. Many leaves, alternate, <u>linear</u>*, light green.

Each of the many yellow flowers—the "butter"—has an orange spot—the "egg"—on the lower lip. At the base of the flower is a spur. The erect stems are 6″ to 2-1/2′ tall; and they grow freely along roadsides, around settlements and in canyons. Plains-Montane. *Linaria vulgaris,* Figwort Family.

*A similar species, *Linaria dalmatica,* has clasping, <u>ovate leaves</u>. Plant may be taller and have larger flowers.

YELLOW MONKEY-FLOWER *(p. 167)*	Bright yellow, 2-lipped flowers (see Key Terms) 1″ long, with closed throat. <u>Red spots on lower lip.</u> Broad, opposite, toothed leaves. In or beside water.

Blossoms may be solitary at top or several along stem. Plant varies in size from 2″ near timberline with flowers 1/2″ long, to 20″ at lower elevations with flowers over 1-1/2″ long. It grows in wet places among rocks and has smooth, weak stems, erect or decumbent. Montane-Subalpine. *Mimulus guttatus,* Figwort Family. The cultivated snapdragon belongs to the Figwort Family.

ST. JOHNSWORT
(p. 167)

> 1″ saucer flowers. 5 petals with tiny black dots near their margins. Showy stamens. Small, opposite, entire leaves also have black dots.

1. **WESTERN ST. JOHNSWORT**—Flowers are few, bright yellow, and scattered over top of plant. The petal margins are strongly dotted with black and the sepals may be, also. Sometimes the dots are clear. The buds may be tinged with red. Leaves, 1/2 to 1″ long, have black dots along the margins; this can be seen by holding a leaf to the light. Plant, 8-24″ tall, has smooth stems and few branches. It prefers damp places. Montane-Subalpine. Jun-Sep. *Hypericum formosum,* St. Johnswort Family.

2. **KLAMATH WEED**—similar to the above, including the black dots, but the flowers are numerous in a broad, flat-topped cluster, and plant is profusely branched. Plains-Foothills. *Hypericum perforatum.*

   There is one important difference. Klamath Weed is poisonous to white livestock. They develop sores and skin itch and become blind, hence may die of starvation. On a black and white animal, the sores develop only on the white part of the skin. Stockmen have been able to control this problem somewhat by importing a certain beetle from Europe which feeds on Klamath Weed but not on crops.

LOUSEWORT
(p. 167)
(color plate p. 139)

> 3/4″, pale yellow, 2-lipped flowers. Lower lip is spreading; upper lip is compressed on the sides and strongly arched. Leaves divided, or fernlike.

1. **PARRY LOUSEWORT**—Flowers are yellow to creamy. Upper lip curves down into a short, straight beak. Leaves are comb-like, divided nearly to the midrib into narrow, even, toothed lobes. Plant is 4-12″ tall, non-hairy. Chiefly alpine. Mont. to New Mex. and Ariz. *Pedicularis parryi,* Figwort Family.

2. **FERNLEAF LOUSEWORT** or **BRACTED LOUSEWORT**—Spike is densely covered with pale yellow flowers interspersed with forked, leaf-like bracts. Sometimes the flowers are turned slightly, giving a twisted appearance to the spike. Leaves, 2-6″ long, are bright green and fernlike. They are chiefly basal, with smaller ones on the stems reducing into the leafy bracts. Plant, 1-3′ tall, grows in moist, subalpine woods and meadows from Montana to Colo. and Utah. *Pedicularis bracteosa,* var. *paysoniana.*

NOTE. This plant might be confused with Giant Lousewort but

162

Giant's flowers are streaked with red and the upper lip almost touches the lower.

3. **CANADA LOUSEWORT or WOOD BETONY**—Flowers are yellow or sometimes reddish and hooded. Leaves have broad lobes and are divided not more than 2/3 of the way to the midrib. Plant grows in the Foothills-Montane zones. *Pedicularis canadensis.*

GOLDEN BANNER or Golden-pea *(p. 167)* *(color plate p. 139)*	3/4″ bright yellow pea flowers (see Key Terms) along top part of erect stem. 3 leaflets, 1-2″ long, at tip of leaf petiole. Stems 1-2′. Dark buds.

A dozen or more very attractive flowers are attached to the stem by short stalks. Where the leaf petioles join the stem, are large leaf-like stipules. Plant has one to several leafy stems; often occurs in patches along slopes. Apr-Jul. Foothills-Montane. Wyo. and Utah south. *Thermopsis divaricarpa,* Pea Family.

FENDLER GROUNDCHERRY *(p. 167)*	5 dull yellow petals and brownish center. Single 3/4″ bell flower hangs from leaf axil. Leaves alternate. Pods like Chinese lanterns.

Leaves are oval to triangular. Plant has leafy stems 6-24″ tall, with a branching, bushy top. Found on dry, rocky ground from Colo. and Utah south. Plains-Foothills. The papery, 1″ pods enclose a yellow, tomato-like berry. Indians gathered these for food. *Physalis fendleri,* Potato Family.

NOTE. Although some of the species are poisonous, the Potato Family includes several important vegetables, such as potatoes, tomatoes, eggplant, sweet peppers, hot peppers and cayenne (but not the black table condiment; it comes from the seeds of an East Indian plant.) The potato family also includes tobacco and petunias.

COMMON MULLEIN or Great Mullein *(p. 168)*	5 rounded petals. 1/2″ saucer flowers along a thick spike 2-7′ tall. Large, entire, pale green, velvety-soft leaves.

Bright yellow flowers are closely attached to the spike. They open a few at a time, starting with the lowest buds. The wide leaves, 4-16″ long, are densely woolly with tangled, yellowish hairs. The first year, mullein develops a soft, pale green, leaf rosette perhaps a foot wide; the second year it sends up the tall, coarse, straight flower stalk.

After the blooming season ends, the stalks linger on for months, looking like skeletons, some straight, others bent and twisted into weird shapes. Mullein was introduced from Europe and has become very common along roadsides and banks. Plains-Foothills. *Verbascum thapsus,* Figwort Family.

NOTE. Mullein leaves are gathered for medicine and skin lotions. The seeds are a valuable source of winter food for birds.

FIELD LOCO	Numerous 3/4″ pea flowers with sharp beak (see Key Terms). Yellow to whitish. Leaves basal. 17-31 leaflets.

Plant 12-20″ tall. Usually on gravelly slopes. Montane-Subalpine. Colo. north. *Oxytropis campestris,* Pea Family.

PRAIRIE CINQUEFOIL *(p. 168)*	5 petals. Crowded clusters of 1/2″ saucer flowers. 5 to 9 pinnate leaflets cut halfway to midrib into crowded, divided lobes; pale below. Sturdy 6-36″ stems.

Leaves are usually divided into 7 leaflets, 1/2 to 2″ long, which in turn, are divided into oblong or linear lobes. They are green above and pale below with matted hairs. The erect stems grow on dry, open fields or hillsides. Foothills-Montane. Both flowers and leaflets are more crowded than on most cinquefoils. *Potentilla pennsylvanica,* Rose Family.

GOLDENROD *(p. 168)*	Large, compact clusters of tiny ray and disk flowers.* Leaves alternate, entire or toothed, but never compound nor lobed. 4 species follow.

All goldenrod flowers are much alike although the size of the cluster varies. The clusters are always grouped along the upper part of the stem, sometimes all on one side.

*Each individual flower or head, about 1/3″ wide, consists of a few small rays and disk flowers. Several of these individual heads are attached to one short stem, forming a small cluster. A number of these clusters are grouped more or less densely around the top or along the side of the main stem, forming a fairly large cluster called the inflorescence.

164

There are over a dozen species of goldenrod in this region, most of them difficult to distinguish. May be 4″ to 6′ tall.

1. **SMOOTH GOLDENROD**—Flower heads are spaced irregularly in a somewhat round-topped, elongated cluster. Often on one side of stem. Leaves are 3-nerved, more or less leathery, have petioles; basal leaves are larger near the tip. The 6-16″ plant is smooth with little or no hair. Plains-Montane. *Solidago missouriensis,* or *concinna,* Composite Family.

2. **ROUGH GOLDENROD**—Flowers may or may not be on one side of stem. Leaves are rather short and are larger near the tip. Plant is densely covered with short hairs. It is common in dry places, in clumps. Plains-Montane. Although it is called Rough Goldenrod and is a very hairy plant, the hairs are not actually stiff nor harsh. *Solidago nana.*

3. **DWARF GOLDENROD**—Flowers usually have 8 very narrow rays in each head. Leaves are toothed around the tips, and have long petioles. The 4-6″ stems are decumbent and reddish. Little or no hair. Subalpine-Alpine, in rocky places. *Solidago spathulata,* var. *nana,* or *Solidago decumbens* .

4. **TALL GOLDENROD**—The large flower cluster is more or less flat-topped but the tiny heads are mainly along one side of the little stems forming the cluster. Leaves are 3-nerved, sharply toothed, and sessile. Stems, 1-1/2 to 4′ tall, are rather leafy and hairy. Found in wet or moist places. Foothills-Montane. *Solidago canadensis.*

NOTES. Goldenrod is the state flower of Nebraska.

Goldenrod pollen is relatively heavy and is distributed by insects instead of wind, hence it seldom causes hay fever.

YELLOW **SWEET-CLOVER** *(p. 168)*	1/4″ pea flowers in long, slender, axillary clusters that may be erect or may droop. Fragrant. 3 leaflets less than 1″ long; toothed. Bushy plant along roads.

Light yellow flowers bloom in loose, finger-like clusters. Plant has sturdy, much branched stems 1-6′ tall. Very common in fields and on roadsides. Plains-Montane. *Melilotus officinalis,* Pea Family.

WHITE SWEET-CLOVER—very similar to the preceding only the flowers are white; and it begins blooming later—in July. *Melilotus alba.*

NOTE. When young, either species of sweet-clover is good forage for livestock, and mule deer like it. Bees make good honey from it.

YELLOW/STALK

165

TANSY MUSTARD
(p. 168)

4 petals. <u>Dense clusters</u> of 1/8″ pale yellow flowers. Leaves lacy; cut into <u>very narrow divisions</u> usually <u>very close together</u>. Erect. Branched.

Small flower clusters at branch tips. Leaves, 2-4″ long, are alternate and appear lacy because they are cut into such fine, close divisions. The stem is 4-30″ tall, hairy, and somewhat rough. It often grows in disturbed ground. Plains-Foothills. Pods are small, narrow and either erect or spreading. *Descurania sophia* and *pinnata,* Mustard Family.

GOLD-TONGUE
or Yellow Owl-clover

1/4″, lemon-yellow flowers; <u>each</u> <u>protrudes</u> 1/8″ from small, dense, green bracts along an erect 4-12″ stem. Narrow leaves, usually entire and sessile.

The little flowers peek out from the bracts, looking as though they are closed or folded. Actually they are irregularly 2-lipped and are not related to clover. Bracts are usually 3-cleft. Leaves are rarely 3-cleft. Common on dry hillsides. Foothills-Montane. *Orthocarpus luteus,* Figwort Family.

Common Evening-primrose

Butter-and-eggs

Yellow Monkey-flower

Western St. Johnswort

Parry Lousewort

Fernleaf Lousewort

Golden Banner

Groundcherry

Common Mullein   **Prairie Cinquefoil**

Smooth Goldenrod   **Dwarf Goldenrod**

Yellow Sweet-clover   **Tansy Mustard**

YELLOW	Cluster 2-4″ long of 1 to 1-1/2″ ver-
PAINTBRUSH	tically overlapping "petals". Small,
(p. 175)	green, pointed tips may protrude
(color plate p. 139)	from these "petals". 3 common
	species are:

1. **NORTHERN PAINTBRUSH**—The "petals" are actually leaf-like bracts that partially or completely hide the true flowers which are small, green and needle-shaped. The bracts may be entire or lobed. If lobed, there is usually a long lobe between 2 short ones. Color is variable; yellow or whitish or greenish, but never reddish-purple. Leaves are alternate and entire or the upper ones may be 3-lobed. The one or more 8-16″ stems are often branched from the base. Common in moist, shady meadows usually below 11,000 feet. Montane-Subalpine. It is slightly hairy around the flowers. *Castilleja sulphurea,* or *septentrionalis,* Figwort Family.
2. **WESTERN PAINTBRUSH**—Flower bracts may be entire or shallowly lobed. They are usually greenish-yellow but sometimes are tinged with reddish-purple. Top of the flower stem is densely hairy. Plant has several unbranched stems, 2-8″ tall and grows in clumps from timberline up, especially on tundra. Colo., Utah and New Mex. *Castilleja occidentalis.*
3. **PLAINS PAINTBRUSH**—Flower bracts, greenish-yellow or whitish, are only slightly hairy. Leaves are linear and entire; upper ones may be divided into linear lobes. This is a spring plant, 4-6″ tall. Plains-Foothills. *Castilleja sessiliflora.*

CREEPING	1-4″ clusters of 1/2″ saucer flowers;
HOLLY-GRAPE	buds like yellow pellets. Holly-like,
or Oregon Grape *(p. 175)*	spine-edged leaves. Shrub 4-12″ tall.

Flowers are sweetly fragrant, and have 6 tiny petals and 6 sepals but unless fully open, they look like little pellets. Berries are dark blue and bitter. Leaves have 3 to 7 leathery, evergreen leaflets. In fall, the leaves turn brilliant red, yellow, rich brown, even purple, and linger on throughout winter. This little creeping, evergreen sub-shrub grows on dry rocky slopes, often near scrub oaks and in partial shade. Foothills-Montane. *Mahonia,* or *Berberis repens,* Barberry Family

NOTES. "Repens" means creeping. The flowers are a favorite of bees. The roots make a fine, yellow dye. The plant is very similar to the state flower of Oregon.

PARRY THISTLE
(p. 175)

One or more yellowish flower puffs in a nest of very cobwebby, spiny bracts. Prickly leaves, green on both sides. Thick, erect, spiny 2-5′ stem.

Flowers are greenish-yellow, pale yellow or brownish-yellow. The overlapping bracts have both spines and fringy hair. Short, narrow leaves extend out below the bracts. The flowers may be single or in clusters, terminal or axillary. Like all thistles the heads are composed of disk flowers only. Plant has a sturdy, grooved stem and is often found near water. Montane-Subalpine. Occurs in Colo. and Utah southward. *Cirsium parryi,* Composite Family.

WESTERN WALLFLOWER
(p. 175)
(color plate p. 142)

4 wide petals. 1 to 2-1/2″ heads of 1/2″ flat flowers; lemon-yellow or dark orange.* Leaves alternate, <u>very narrow,</u> slightly rough.

Flowers are yellow, and bloom—usually—in dense, rounded fragrant clusters. Leaves may be entire or toothed. The plant is 2-24″ tall with one or more rather rough stems. The long slender pods are 4-angled and either spread out or turn up. Foothills-Subalpine. *Erysimum asperum* and *inconspicuum,* Mustard Family.

*****WHEELER WALLFLOWER**—is almost identical with the preceding only the flowers are orange or maroon color. Foothills-Alpine. Chiefly Colo., New Mex. and Ariz. *Erysimum wheeleri.*

ALPINE WALLFLOWER—is also very similar to the preceding. It is 2-6″ tall, has lemon-yellow flowers; sometimes lavender or pink. Alpine only. Colo. and Utah. *Erysimum nivale.*

NOTE. Wallflower belongs to the very large Mustard Family which includes numerous flowers, many weeds, and some well-known vegetables, such as: cabbage, radishes, turnips, kale, cauliflower, horseradish, rutabaga, watercress. The mustard of commerce is made from the ground seeds of some members of this family.

SULPHUR-FLOWER
or Umbrella Plant
(p. 175)

1 to 2-1/2″ umbel of 1/8″ flowers. Leafy bracts circle base of umbel. Leafless stems rise from mat of <u>entire,</u> green leaves, usually silvery below.

The tiny bright yellow flowers (see Creamy Sulphur-flower next) are closely packed in an umbel where the pedicels branch out like the spokes of a miniature, open umbrella. Leafy, drooping bracts circle the base of the umbel. The flowers linger indefinitely and as they mature, may change to shades of orange, maroon or brown. The thick-textured leaves, 1/2 to 1-1/2″ long, oval to oblong, form a green mat. The several stems are stout, hairy and 4-12″ tall. Sulphur-flower is common on open, dry slopes. Foothills-Subalpine. Wyo. south. *Eriogonum umbellatum,* Buckwheat Family.

CREAMY SULPHUR-FLOWER or Subalpine Buckwheat—is very similar to the above but its flowers are cream color, turning to rose. Abundant in the Subalpine zone. Colo. north. *Eriogonum subalpinum.*

HARES-EAR MUSTARD	4 narrow petals. 2/3″ flowers. Leaves alternate, broad, oblong, sessile, and clasp stem, usually with little ears. Very slender pods. Erect 1-2′ stem.

Flowers pale yellow to whitish. Pods 3-4″ long, turn up. Plains-Foothills. Colo. north. *Conringia orientalis,* Mustard Family.

TAPERLEAF or Golden Shower	Small heads of disk flowers only. Leaves opposite, triangular, with slender points like tails 2-5″ long.

Light yellow flower heads. Bushy plant 2-5′. Jul-Oct. Rocky foothills. Colo., New Mex. and Ariz. *Pericome caudata,* Composite Family.

YELLOW PARSLEY *(p. 176)* *(color plate p. 141)*	1/2 to 2″ umbel of tiny lemon-yellow (may be greenish-yellow) flowers with protruding stamens. Few alternate, much divided leaves. Petioles sheathe stem. Plant 3″ (or 1″) to 30″ tall. 3 common species are:

1. **WHISKBROOM PARSLEY**—Flowers are in a double umbel i.e. the larger umbel, 1-2″ wide, is composed of small umbels 1/2″ or less. These umbels are often flat. Flowers may bloom as plant comes up. The fine, linear divisions of the leaves do not narrow at the ends. Like all members of the Carrot Family, the base of the leaf petiole is enlarged and sheathes the plant stem. Plant, 3-20″, is abundant in spring on rather dry fields and hillsides. Foothills-Montane. Wyo. and Utah south. *Harbouria trachypleura,* Carrot Family.

2. **YELLOW MOUNTAIN PARSLEY** or **Wild Yellow Parsley**—Flowers are like those above. The leaf divisions are a little wider than those of Whiskbroom Parsley and the lobes look slightly like deer antlers. More important—they <u>are narrowed at the ends</u>. Plant, 8-30″ tall, likes moist meadows and woods in the higher mountains, especially subalpine. Occurs Wyo. and Utah southwards. *Pseudocymopterus montanus.*
(p. 176)

3. **ALPINE PARSLEY**—These wee, yellow or sometimes greenish flowers are in compact umbels 1/4 to 1/2″ wide. There is <u>no plant stem</u> so the tiny, much dissected leaves are all basal. These little sod-forming plants—1/2 to 4″ high—are common on gravelly soil at high altitudes. Utah and Wyo. south. *Oreoxis alpina.*

NOTE. These species are related to the garden parsley which is used as a garnish for food.

STONECROP *(p. 176)*	1″ clusters of <u>star flowers</u>; <u>pointed petals</u>. Yellow stamens. Leaves basal and alternate; <u>linear, fleshy</u>. Plant 1-8″. Non-hairy.

The little stars are in crowded clusters; each flower with 5 (or 4) petals. The 1/2″, pointed leaves look like plump, little fleshy bodies close to the stem. (A fleshy leaf is round in cross-section instead of flat.) Leaf color varies from green to reddish-brown, rarely yellow. A leaf rosette appears first; then the flower stem. Plant can thrive with a minimum of water because the fleshy leaves are adapted to store moisture for dry periods and they have a waxy covering which prevents evaporation. Plains-Alpine. In sunny, rocky ground. *Sedum lanceolatum* or *stenopetalum,* Stonecrop Family.

YELLOW-CRESS	4 tiny petals. Small flower clusters at <u>top of branches with pods forming below</u>. Leaves alternate; much divided. <u>Erect, branched stem</u>. Wet places.

Flowers about 1/3″. The petals are longer than the sepals. Plant 4-16″. On roadsides or low damp spots. Plains-Foothills. This is one of several similar yellow species. *Rorippa sinuata,* Mustard Family.

YELLOW/HEAD

MOUNTAIN BLADDERPOD *(p. 176)*	4 lemon-yellow petals. 1″ clusters of 1/4″ saucer flowers on tips of <u>decumbent stems</u> 2-8″ long. Leaves basal and alternate; small and silvery with petioles. Inflated pods. Dry, sandy soil.

Flowers are numerous on the turned-up tips of spreading stems. Plant may start blooming while it is still very small and compact. Petals are widely separated. The pedicels are definitely S-shaped. Leaves, entire or toothed, are in a basal rosette, with a few scattered along the stems. Plant has hairy, grayish stems and grows on road banks and dry, sandy soil. Wyo. to New Mex. The seed pod is inflated like a bladder: hence the name, bladderpod. Foothills-Montane. *Lesquerella montana,* Mustard Family.

TWINPOD—Flowers and plant are very similar to the preceding but the <u>pods are double.</u> Twinpod is often a more compact plant. *Physaria australis* and others, Mustard Family. One species, FIDDLE-LEAF TWINPOD, occurs only on Colorado foothills and can be recognized by the double bladder pod and by small, fiddle-shaped leaves. *Physaria vitulifera.*

MOUNTAIN CARAWAY	3/4″ <u>umbels</u> of tiny, yellow flowers. No plant stem. <u>All leaves basal,</u> and divided into a dense, green mass of ovate leaflets.

The leaflets flare out and are toothed or divided again. Plant 2-14″. Rocky foothills in spring. Colo. to Tex. and Mexico. *Aletes acaulis,* Carrot Family.

DRABA *(p. 176)*	4 rounded petals. Head of small, flat flowers at top or along the sides of a short, <u>erect stem rising from a leaf rosette.</u> Leaves basal; often alternate, too; narrow, entire or toothed.

There are many species of draba in this region. Accurate identification depends upon the pods but most drabas share the above characteristics. The word "draba" comes from the Greek, <u>drabe</u>—mustard.

    The tiny, bright yellow petals form a cross. Near timberline draba is only 1″ or 2″ tall; in lower altitudes it may be 2-10″. Most drabas are hairy, and some species have white flowers.

1. **GOLDEN DRABA**—usually has several 2-6″ stems with many flowers; the leaves are wider near the end; and the pods are slightly twisted. Montane-Subalpine. *Draba aurea,* Mustard Family.
2. **TWISTED POD DRABA**—is similar but has definitely twisted pods. Colo. to New Mex. *Draba aurea,* Mustard Family.
3. **THICK-LEAVED DRABA**—no leaves on the stem. *Draba crassifolia.*
4. **SHINY DRABA**—has smooth, shiny leaves; stems may be branched. Colo. north. *Draba stenoloba.*

MUSTARDS

Small clusters of little yellow flowers with 4 petals arranged like a cross. Alternate leaves.

There are numerous species of little yellow—or white—mustard flowers similar to Draba. It is hard to distinguish between them, and many have no common names. Most of them differ from Draba in:

1. having no basal rosette;
2. blooming along little,branched, side stems, instead of just at the top or close to the sides of the main plant stem.

Sometimes their leaf bases clasp the plant stem and sometimes the foliage is slightly rough-hairy.

Westerm Paintbursh

Creeping Holly-grape

Parry Thistle

Wallflower

Sulphur-flower

Whiskbroom Parsley

Yellow Mountain Parsley

Stonecrop

Mountain Bladderpod

Draba

EVENING-STAR (See White/Saucer)	2-4″ (or 6″) star flowers, usually white, sometimes pale yellow. Usually 10 petals. Many stamens. A few rough, alternate, "clingy" leaves. Open in late afternoon.

YELLOW POND-LILY *(p. 188)*	2-4″ waxy, cuplike flowers. Large, shiny leaves float on surface of lakes.

The bright yellow flowers float on the surface of the water or may lie just below it. The 3 to 12 showy, yellow sepals are often tinged with red. Numerous petals, much smaller, are nearly hidden by the many stamens. Leaves are entire, rounded to ovate, and 6-16″ long. They lie flat on the surface of quiet water. Strong stems support the flowers which rise from large yellowish rootstalks that may twist along the floor of the lake or may lie embedded in the mud. Plant is common in the cold water of montane and subalpine lakes. Colorado to Alaska. *Nuphar luteum* sp. *polysepalum,* Waterlily Family.

NOTES. This is one of the few plants that are represented in this area by only one species.

Indians ate the roasted seeds, called "wokas"; they taste like popcorn.

YELLOW STEMLESS EVENING-PRIMROSE *(p. 188)* *(color plate p. 141 and on cover)*	4 large, rounded petals.Bright yellow flower 2-4″ wide. Long yellow stamens. Basal leaves only; lance-shaped. Plant 3-5″ high.

The fragrant flowers open in the evening and wither in bright sunlight turning to old-rose color. There is no plant stem but the 4 narrow sepals end in a stem-like tube 2-6″ long. (See Note under Common Evening-Primrose, in Yellow/Stalk.) Plant is a rosette with long, narrow, dark green leaves, usually toothed. It grows on shale banks. Foothills. *Oenothera brachycarpa,* Evening-Primrose Family.

HUNGER CACTUS or Prickly Pear Cactus *(p. 188)*	1-1/2 to 3″, cuplike flower on edge of cactus pad. Many wide, waxy petals, many stamens, large green pistil. No leaves. Prickly, pad-like stems.

The stamens and pistil are in a cuplike nest of satiny, yellow petals that turn orange when they fade. Although broad, each petal has a tiny spine-like tip and there are reddish streaks at their base. NO

LEAVES. The functions that are accomplished by leaves in other plants are carried on by the green stems of the prickly pear cacti. The stems are actually flat, oval to round, fleshy pads called <u>joints</u>. These joints are 2-6″ long and are joined together, side by side, like so many plates. Sharp spines are arranged on the joints in definite patterns. These fleshy joints can store water to sustain the plant during long dry periods and they are thickly coated with wax to prevent evaporation of the stored water. Most prickly pear cacti in the area from Colorado northward are not over 8″ high. Plains-Foothills. Any adequate description of the many and varied cacti in New Mexico and Arizona is outside the scope of this book. *Opuntia polyacantha,* Cactus Family.

NOTES. Two or three other species of Prickly Pear Cactus found in this region may have yellow, pink or copper-colored flowers.

Prickly Pear fruit is edible—if the hungry traveler has enough patience to remove all the spines! It is native in 45 states, but grows best in Mexico which is the cactus center of the world.

The name, Prickly Pear, is applied to species which have <u>flat, plate-like, jointed stems</u>, like the Hunger Cactus. Most cacti with round stems joined <u>like links of sausage</u>, are called Chollas (CHAW yas) and they grow from New Mexico and Arizona southwards.

EVENING-STAR
(p. 188)

1-1/2 to 3″ yellow star flowers; 5—or 10—pointed petals. Many long, showy <u>stamens</u>. Long, rough "clingy" <u>leaves</u>. On dry banks. 2 common yellow species follow.

The leaves are covered with stiff, barbed hairs which give them a texture like fine sandpaper, enabling them to stick to clothing. Most of the leaves are pinnately divided into lobes that may be toothed or entire. Plants are common on sandy banks and roadsides. W   New Mex. Plains-Foothills.

1. **YELLOW EVENING-STAR**—Flowers are <u>1-1/2 to 2-1/2″ wide,</u> and usually have 10 petals. They open late in the afternoon and close the following forenoon. During the day, the plant looks weedy and unattractive but in late afternoon, the blossoms open out into beautiful yellow stars. Plant, 1 to 2-1/2′ tall, is much branched. *Mentzelia speciosa* or *multiflora,* Loasa Family.

2. **SMALL-FLOWERED STICKLEAF or SMALL-FLOWERED MENTZELIA**—Flowers are about <u>1/2″ wide,</u> with <u>5 petals</u>. They <u>bloom during the daytime.</u> The slender stems, 4-16″ tall, are <u>shiny white</u>. *Mentzelia albicaulis.*

178

ORIENTAL	4 long "petals", slender, <u>widely</u>
CLEMATIS	separated. 1-1/2″ flowers on
or Yellow Clematis	<u>spreading vine.</u> Leaves opposite with
(p. 188)	leaflets. Wiry, angled stems.

Flowers are often nodding and may occur singly or a few on long stalks. Usually are so numerous that the vine is loaded with yellow flowers, sometimes tinged with green. There are 4 pointed petal-like sepals but no true petals. The leaflets are lobed or coarsely toothed. Plant is a leafy vine, 10-20′ long, with slender, spreading, tangled stems. In fall, there are silvery seed plumes. Foothills. *Clematis orientalis,* Buttercup Family.

COMMON	4 wide petals. 1-1/2″ flower. Long
EVENING-PRIMROSE	stamens and long pistil with rod-like
(See Yellow/Stalk)	tips. <u>Sepals turn down.</u> Leaves alter-
	nate, <u>lance-shaped.</u> Stem 6″ to 3′ tall.

GLOBEFLOWER	1-1/4″ creamy flowers, one on each
(p. 188)	stalk. 5 to 15 "petals". <u>Also tiny</u>
	<u>petals.</u>* Leaves <u>have large, toothed,</u>
	<u>palmate lobes.</u> Non-hairy. <u>Wet</u>
	<u>places.</u>

*The pale yellow or cream-colored flowers may fade to dingy white. The "petals" are actually sepals. The real petals, at their base, are very tiny and encircle the numerous yellow stamens and several pistils. Plant is leafy, non-hairy, and 6-20″ tall. Globeflowers grow in marshy places, usually in clumps and often near White Marsh-marigolds. Chiefly subalpine. Colorado northward. *Trollius laxus var. albiflorus,* Buttercup Family.

NOTE. Globeflower might be confused with Anemones but all anemones are quite hairy and they have a whorl of leaflike bracts circling the stem one to several inches below the flower. Also, anemones have no real petals.

SALSIFY	1-1/2″ lemon-yellow flower, strap-
or Oyster Plant	shaped rays only; center rays shorter.
or Goatsbeard	Long, <u>projecting bracts.</u> Grass-like
(p. 188)	leaves <u>clasp stem.</u>

Flowers open in the forenoon. The long, narrow bracts sometimes point almost straight up, forming a cup. (In another species, rays and bracts are of equal length.) Attached to each ray can be seen a brown, thread-like style bearing 2 tiny yellow stigmas. Stem, 8-36″ tall, is erect and contains a milky juice. Salsify's most conspicuous feature is the delicate, round seed head which looks very much like the dandelion seed head but is larger—up to 4″ in diam.—and tops a taller plant. Each seed is attached to a silky tuft which, if examined in sunlight, shimmers like threads of gold. *Tragopogon dubius,* Composite Family.

DANDELION *(p. 188)*	Solitary flower, 3/4 to 2″, of rays only, center ones shorter. All leaves in a basal rosette. Plant low, but the leafless flowering stem is 2-24″. See 5 common species below.

All have milky juice, and all have the pappus which becomes a round seed head like that of the familiar dandelion. (For pappus, see drawing of Composite Flower.) Rays are strap-shaped and toothed, and the central ones are shorter than the outer rays which tends to make the head flat. A close look will show the thread-like style with 2 stigmas (like 2 branches) which often droop gracefully. This is true, not only of dandelions but of most composites. A stigma is the part of a flower that receives the pollen which then passes down the style to the tiny ovary at the base of the ray.

1. **COMMON DANDELION**—Flower is 1-2″ wide. A row of <u>inner bracts point up</u>; the <u>outer bracts curve down</u>. Leaves are lance-shaped and 2-15″ long, with edges variously cut and lobed. There is no plant stem. The dandelion is found in all zones, and it blooms throughout the flowering season—March-October. *Taraxacum officinale,* Composite Family.

NOTES. The name, dandelion, comes from the French <u>dent-de-lion</u>, lion's tooth, referring to the leaf shape. Originally a native of Eurasia, the dandelion has become probably the most universal of all plants; and, due to its propensity for lawns, one of the most detested. In reality, it is a useful plant. Young leaves are used as "greens" and in salads, also for tea. Wine can be made from the flowers. Medicine is obtained from the large, fleshy roots, and they may also be used in salads.

The dandelion is an excellent source of food for wildlife, such as grouse, wild geese, elk, deer, porcupines, and bears.

2. **FALSE DANDELION**—looks just like the common dandelion but the bracts overlap, are brown or purplish with light streaks, and <u>they all point up.</u> Leaves may be lobed, toothed or entire. Plant can grow in drier places than the preceding. Foothills-Alpine. *Agoseris glauca.*

3. **BURNT-ORANGE DANDELION or ORANGE AGOSERIS**—Flower is much like the above only it is smaller—usually 3/4″—and is a <u>deep orange color</u>, sometimes

180

drying to light purplish. The leaves are dark green and linear or wider at the ends; entire, toothed or lobed. Flower stem is 4-24″. Foothills-Alpine. *Agoseris aurantiaca.*

4. **WAVY-LEAF DANDELION**—Flower looks much like the common dandelion only the rays may be fewer and wider and are generally reddish on the back. Leaves are entire and linear; often have white-hairy edges. Plant usually 2-6″, and blooms Apr-Jun. Plains-Foothills. *Nothocalais cuspidata.*

5. **TUNDRA DANDELION**—looks just like the common dandelion but the outer bracts have little, horn-shaped swellings at the tips. Plant, usually 2 or 3″ high (to 10″) is found from Alaska to New Mexico and is circumpolar on grassy tundra. *Taraxacum ceratophorum.*

ALPINE ANEMONE (See White/Saucer)	4 to 7 "petals", not veined. 1″ pale saucer flower; one or more rise from a wide, leafy collar circling the plant stem. No green sepals. Leaves deeply divided.
PACIFIC ANEMONE (See Red/Saucer)	One cup-shape flower 1″ deep, tops a slender stem. 5 to 9 "petals". Leaves deeply cut into narrow parts. Hairy plant under 12″. Seed pods like thimbles.
BUFFALO-BUR	5 pointed, yellow petals. 5 sepals. 1″ irregular, saucer flowers. Leaves alternate, lobed* and prickly. Stem 6-28″ and spiny.

*Leaf lobes are rounded between, and at their ends. Branched plant has long yellow spines. Fruits are spiny burs. Plains-Foothills. Fields and waste places. North Dak. to Wyo. and south to Mexico. *Solanum rostratum.* Potato Family.

BUTTERCUPS *(p. 189)* *(color plate p. 142)*	1/3″ to 1-1/2″ bright yellow, waxy flowers. Usually 5 petals (one species has up to 10). Many stamens surround a small, greenish cone. 7 common species follow.

Buttercups can be recognized by the shiny, waxed or varnished appearance of the yellow flowers but some of the more than 30 species found in this region are hard to identify. The cone-like center might be confused with the Daisy Shape flowers but, unlike the Daisy group, buttercup cones are surrounded by many separate, freely-moving stamens.

1. **SNOW BUTTERCUP or ALPINE BUTTERCUP**—Flowers, 1 to 1-1/2″, resemble poppies; may open before the leaves unfold. All leaves are divided into thread-like parts. This 1-8″ plant grows in the alpine zone only, where it is often found beside melting snow or even pushing up thru it. Wyo., Utah and Colo. *Ranunculus adoneus,* Buttercup Family.

2. **MACAULEY BUTTERCUP**—has 1″ flowers; black (or reddish-brown) hairy sepals; and leaves 1″ broad at end with 3 teeth at the tip—sometimes more, but usually 3. Alpine only. *Ranunculus macauleyi,* Colo. and New Mex.

3. **HEART-LEAVED BUTTERCUP**—1″ flowers. Leaves are of 2 kinds; some basal leaves are heart-shaped, with long stalks; the upper stem leaves are divided into linear lobes. Plant, 6-16″ tall, is hairy, and grows in moist meadows. Montane-Subalpine. *Ranunculus cardiophyllus.*

4. **CALTHA-FLOWERED BUTTERCUP**—3/4″ flowers, have 10 petals (rarely 5 to 9). All leaves are undivided and usually entire. Plant, 4-12″ tall, may be branched above. Found in moist meadows, chiefly in subalpine zone. Wyo. thru Colo. - *Ranunculus alismaefolius.*

5. **SAGEBRUSH BUTTERCUP**—This is the first buttercup to appear in spring—Mar. to June. 3/4″ flower. The small sepals are tinged with lavender. Leaves are of 2 kinds; basal ones are entire and rather thick-textured; some of the stem leaves are 3-lobed with the middle lobe largest. Plant is 2-8″, is non-hairy, and like most buttercups, it prefers moist locations. Foothills-Montane. *Ranunculus glaberrimus.*

6. **SHORE BUTTERCUP**—1/3″ flowers; leaves are rounded and scalloped; and plant has runners, that is, trailing shoots that develop roots. It creeps on wet ground or muddy shores beside water. Plains-Montane. *Ranunculus cymbalaria.*

7. **SPEARWORT**—like the above only the leaves are entire, and very narrow. Montane-Subalpine. Colo. north. *Ranunculus flammula.*

CINQUEFOIL or Potentilla	5 rounded petals. 1/4 to 1″ flowers. Pointed, green sepal tips show between the petals. Calyx has 10 parts.* Sepals do not droop. 3 to 17 toothed leaflets (only one, a prostrate species, has up to 31). Has leaf-like stipules (small appendages at the base of the leaf petiole).

There are many cinquefoils (potentillas) in Western United States.

They belong to the rose family. The plants vary considerably but the flowers are all very similar. 11 species are included in this book. The 5 heart-shaped petals are usually yellow and in some species have an orange spot at their bases. There are 5 pointed sepals; *5 smaller "bractlets" alternate with these sepals, thus making 10 parts in the calyx. This distinguishes cinquefoils from buttercups which have only 5 parts in the calyx—the 5 sepals.

Cinquefoil (SINK foil) leaves are always compound, with leaflets either pinnate (along both sides of the midrib) or palmate (leaflets at the tip of the midrib, like fingers). Following are 4 common species with pinnate leaflets:

1. **LEAFY CINQUEFOIL or LEAFY POTENTILLA or WOOD BEAUTY**—Flowers are usually 1″ wide, and creamy to bright yellow. Leaves have 9 to 13 green, sharply toothed, hairy leaflets that decrease progressively in size towards the base of the leaf. Very small leaflets are often interspersed among the regular ones. Leaves may be sticky. There are several erect, sturdy, hairy stems 8-12″ tall. Plant is common, often growing near rocks. Foothills-Subalpine. So. Dak. and Wyo. to New Mex. *Potentilla fissa. (p. 189)*

2. **SILVERWEED**—Flowers are 3/4″ wide, and bright yellow; each blossom solitary on a rather long stem. Leaves are like delicate ferns and may have as many as 31 toothed leaflets interspersed with smaller ones. They are silvery-white beneath and may be green or silvery on top. Plant is prostrate, in wet places. It spreads by long runners, usually red, which root at the tips. Plains-Subalpine. *Potentilla anserina. (p. 189)*

3. **SILVERY CINQUEFOIL or SILVERY POTENTILLA**—Lemon-yellow flowers are 1/2″ wide. The 5 to 13 toothed leaflets are silvery on both sides. The graceful, leafy stem, 6-20″ tall, may be upright or somewhat leaning. Common on dry ground where it often grows in large colonies. Foothills-Montane. *Potentilla hippiana.*

4. **RIVER CINQUEFOIL**—Flowers, about 1/4″ wide, usually have 10 stamens. The petals are shorter than the sepals. Upper leaves have 3 leaflets; lower ones have 5. The leaflets are wider towards the tips and have coarse teeth. Plant, 6-20″ tall, is erect, finely hairy, and grows in valleys and along lake shores. Plains-Foothills. *Potentilla rivalis.*

> 3 Cinquefoil species with palmate leaflets follow (spread out from tip of petiole.)

5. **GOLDCUP CINQUEFOIL or GOLDCUP POTEN-TILLA**—Flowers, 1/2″ wide, bloom at ends of branches at top of plant. Each petal has a gold spot. The few leaves have 5 to 7 leaflets, both sides greenish. Plant stem is graceful—that is, not stiffly erect—hence the botanical name, gracilis. It is 6-24″ tall, is branched at top and grows on meadows and open slopes. Montane-Subalpine. Colo. to Alaska. *Potentilla gracilis. (p. 189)*

CINQUEFOIL (Potentilla) Hybrids

There is much hybridization between Goldcup and Silvery Cinquefoil which results in: Flowers with or without gold spots; Leaves usually green above and silvery below; Leaflets usually arranged pinnately. All 3—Goldcup, Silvery Cinquefoil, and the hybrids—are very common. Cinquefoil flowers close at night.

6. **ELEGANT CINQUEFOIL**—Few flowers, not crowded. 5 (or 7) palmate leaflets, white-felty beneath, and usually toothed only above the middle. Plant is generally 2-4″ high. Common in dry, rocky places. Foothills-Alpine. Colo. and Utah north. *Potentilla concinna.*

7. **ALPINE CINQUEFOIL or SNOW CINQUEFOIL**—One to several 1/2″ flowers. Leaves have 3 leaflets, densely white-hairy beneath; green or whitish above. Plant, usually 2-6″, has matted hair. Common on tundra and high mountains from Colo. north. This is a circumpolar plant of cold regions. *Potentilla nivea and ledebouriana.*

> A few Cinquefoil species may have either pinnate or palmate leaflets. One of these follows:

8. **BLUELEAF CINQUEFOIL**—A few to several bright, 1/2″ flowers. Leaves, mostly basal, have 5 (or 7) leaflets, toothed above middle. The 2 lowest leaflets are very close to the upper ones. All leaves are blue-green or gray-green on both sides. Stems, generally not over 1′ long, are spreading—not erect. Common in moist mountain meadows. Subalpine-Alpine. *Potentilla diversifolia. (p. 189)*

ALPINE AVENS *(p. 189)*	5 rounded, bright yellow petals. 1″ flower. Calyx has 10 parts. Pointed <u>sepals may be green or purple or brown</u>. Leaves <u>mostly basal</u> with 9 to 33 dark green, non-shiny, pinnate leaflets. The few stem leaves are <u>very much smaller</u>. Often forms a dense mat 2-12″ high.

Sepal tips show plainly between the petal ends. The leaflets have small lobes· or teeth, and in August, they turn bronze or maroon. This is one of the most abundant flowers above timberline—very common on tundra. *Geum rossii,* or *turbinatum,* Rose Family.

NOTE. Alpine Avens might be confused with Cinquefoils but—

ALPINE AVENS	**CINQUEFOILS**
Basal leaves are very numerous, are <u>dark green both sides</u>, have 9 to 33 leaflets, and often form mats.	Some or no basal leaves; green or whitish. Most species have fewer than 17 leaflets. <u>Do not form mats.</u>
Sepals may be green, purplish or brown.	<u>Sepals are always green.</u>

BUR AVENS *(p. 189)*	5 bright petals. 1/2″ flowers; calyx has 10 parts. Sepals soon droop. <u>End leaflet is largest.</u> Erect, 1-3′ <u>stem has bristly hairs</u> but is not spiny. Fruits are prickly burs.

Sepals may be purplish and they droop after bud opens. Leaves have 5 (3 to 7) principal leaflets alternating with smaller ones. The terminal leaflet is larger and is rounded to kidney-shaped. <u>Leaves are not bristly.</u> The stem—or stems—have bristly hair. Bur Avens grows in meadows and damp places. Foothills-Montane. *Geum macrophyllum,* Rose Family.

NOTE. Bur Avens looks very much like cinquefoils but the drooping sepals, the large end leaflet, and the bristly hair on the stem distinguish it.

FRINGED PUCCOON *(p. 190)*	5 fringed petals *Flowers with tube <u>3/4″ long</u>. Many alternate leaves, entire and narrow to linear.

The lemon-yellow petals are toothed or fringed. Flower branches tend to lean so that the flowers usually face to the side instead of upward. Plant has several stems 4-18" tall and is common on dry soil in the spring. Plains-Montane. *Lithospermum incisum,* Borage Family.

*MANY-FLOWERED PUCCOON—is like the preceding but the petals are smaller and have <u>no fringe</u>. *Lithospermum multiflorum,* Wyo. to Mexico.

YELLOW VIOLET or Johny-Jump-Up or Wild Pansy *(p. 190)*	5 petals. 1/2" flower with <u>crook in stem neck</u>. Lowest petal has purplish lines and becomes <u>a spur in back</u>.

The petal backs are often shaded bronze or purple. A small crook at top of the flower stem usually causes the violet to face slightly downward, hence the expression, "modest violet". Leaves are toothed or entire; longer than wide. Plant, 1-3" high, is one of the earliest spring flowers. Apr-Jun. Plains-Subalpine. *Viola nuttallii,* Violet Family. Violets are related to pansies.

NOTE. This violet and a number of other plant species were named for Thomas Nuttall, originally a printer in England, who became an American botanist and naturalist.

Any flower whose species name ends in <u>i</u> or <u>ii</u> was named for a botanist or other well-known person. Parryi for Charles Parry who especially collected Colorado flowers; grayi for Asa Gray, a physician who abandoned medicine to devote his life to botany; fremontii for John Fremont, U.S. army engineer, who helped chart the frontier, and collected many flower specimens for botanical study.

DANDELION **HAWKSBEARD** *(p. 190)*	1/2" yellow dandelion-like heads of rays only. <u>Bracts thickened at base and along their midribs</u>. Leaves variable.*

*Leaves may be entire or toothed; usually some resemble dandelion leaves. The stem leaves are much smaller and alternate. The sturdy stem, 8-20" tall, has milky juice. Plant is variable and common; prefers moist meadows. Plains-Subalpine. *Crepis runcinata,* Composite Family.

YELLOW **WOODSORREL** *(p. 190)*	5 lemon-yellow petals. 1/2" flower. Alternate, <u>clover-like leaves</u> with 3 leaflets. Dainty plant, 2-14".

Often only 2 or 3 flowers at top of plant. Leaves are usually bright green, rarely deep red; with a pleasantly sour taste. Stems erect or ascending, may or may not be branched. Grows in fields and woods. Foothills-Montane. One species is a common weed in gardens. *Oxalis stricta,* Woodsorrel Family.

GOLDEN SAXIFRAGE or Fairy Saxifrage *(p. 190)*	5 golden petals with orange dots. 3/8″ flower. Leaves in basal rosette; also tiny leaves on the 1-3″ stem. Yellow pistil turns red. Alpine.

Flower is rather large for the plant. The yellow pistil turns bright red as it ripens into the pod. Plant usually grows in clumps on tundra. New Mex. and Colo. *Saxifraga serpyllifolia,* or *chrysantha,* Saxifrage Family.

TUMBLE MUSTARD or Jim Hill Mustard *(p. 190)*	4 widely separated petals. 1/4″ pale yellow saucer flowers at branch ends. Stem leaves thread-like but not thick. Bushy. 1-4′.

Flowers are usually numerous—pale yellow to whitish. Early in the season there is a basal leaf-rosette similar to that of a dandelion but this withers early. Stem leaves are very narrow with a few slim lobes. Plant is a stout-stemmed tumbleweed. Was introduced from Europe; is now common on roadsides and vacant lots. Pods are 2-4″ long and very slim. *Sisymbrium altissium,* Mustard Family.

NOTE. Plant is believed to have spread into the West during construction of the first railroad. Jim Hill was an early railroad magnate.

PRICKLY LETTUCE or Compass Plant *(p. 190)*	Pale yellow flowers 1/4″ wide, of rays only, like dandelions. Leaves alternate, deeply cut, with spiny edges; white midrib spiny below. Plant 1-5′.

Heads are numerous although only a few open at one time. May turn bluish in age. Leaves, 1-10″ long, have prickly margins, taper to a point, and often clasp the stem. When growing in the open, the leaves turn so as to be vertical with the edges pointing north and south; hence the name, "compass plant". This is a common weed in fields and gardens and it hybridizes with cultivated lettuce. Jun-Sep. Plains. *Lactuca scariola,* Composite Family.

SIBBALDIA (See Other Colors/Saucer)	5 separated petals framed by green sepals. 1/8″ flower. Tiny clover-like leaves. Plant flat on ground, (rarely to 5″ high).

YELLOW/SAUCER

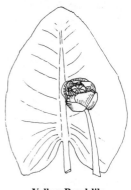

Yellow Pond-lily

Yellow Stemless Evening-primrose

Hunger Cactus (Prickly Pear Cactus)

Small-flowered Stickleaf (Evening-star)

Oriental Clematis

Globeflower

Salsify

Common Dandelion

False Dandelion

Snow Buttercup

Sagebrush Buttercup

Shore Buttercup

Leafy Cinquefoil

Silverweed

Goldcup

Blueleaf Cinquefoil

Alpine Avens

Bur Avens

Fringed Puccoon   **Yellow Violet**   **Dandelion Hawksbeard**

Yellow Woodsorrel   **Golden Saxifrage**   **Tumble Mustard**

Prickly Lettuce

CREEPING HOLLY-GRAPE (See Yellow/Head)	1-4" clusters of 1/2" saucer flowers; buds like yellow pellets. Holly-like spine-edged leaves. Shrub 4-12" tall.

SNOW-LILY or Avalanche-lily or Glacier-lily, or Dog-tooth Violet *(p. 194)*	Please protect! 1-1/2" <u>hanging flower</u>. 6 petals and sepals <u>turn back</u>, exposing 6 long stamens and a greenish pistil. Only 2 leaves, basal, shiny.

Beautiful, bright yellow flower with 3 petals and 3 sepals all alike and strongly recurved. Snow-lily may bloom at the very edge of a melting snow-bank. Plant, 6-15" tall, often grows in clumps, and is more common on the Western Slope, from Colorado northward. Montane-Alpine. It is a favorite food of wild animals. *Erythronium grandiflora,* Lily Family.

YELLOW LADY-SLIPPER *(p. 194)*	Please protect! Lower, sac-like petal is greatly inflated; looks like toe of slipper; about 1" long. Other 2 petals are narrow and <u>twisted</u>, with brownish streaks.

This is an orchid and it is in grave danger of extinction. Orchids have 3 petals, 3 sepals (2 or them joined except near tips), and a column of stamens and pistil fused together. Flower is usually solitary. The slipper toe is bright yellow with a greenish sheen. It attracts insects and serves as a landing pad for them. Long, broad leaves enclose the lower part of stem.

    Plant is an endangered species, having been almost exterminated by being picked. Its leafy stem, 8-20" tall, grows in moist, aspen groves. Montane-Subalpine. *Cypripedium calceolus,* var. *pubescens,* Orchid Family.

NOTES. These plants can be obtained from eastern nurseries without digging any of the few remaining here, and they grow well in cultivation which many wild flowers do not. Also they bloom earlier.

    The botanical name, Cypripedium, comes from Greek words meaning, "Aphrodite" and "sandal". Later this became "Our Lady's Slipper". Calceolus means "little shoe".

191

GOLDEN SMOKE
or Golden Corydalis
(p. 194)

Clusters of 3/4" flowers. 4 slim, very irregular, lemon-yellow petals. Small, tube-like spur.* Bluish feathery foliage. Low clump.

*Flowers are "bird-like" with 2 tiny sepals and 4 petals. The outer 2 petals spread and one has a 1/4" spur; the inner 2 petals are joined at the tips and enclose the stamens. The bluish-green leaves are delicately cut. The tuft of short, spreading stems grows in moist places or disturbed soil like road banks. Sometimes the clump is almost covered with flowers; in other cases the fine-textured foliage forms the center of the clump while yellow flowers peek out around the edge, near the ground or resting upon it. Plains-Montane. Alaska to New Mex. and Calif. *Corydalis aurea,* Fumitory Family.

NOTES. Plant received its name because some species have a smoke-like odor. The cultivated Bleeding Heart belongs to this family.

YELLOWBELLS
or Yellow Fritillary

6 lobes. 1" bell-flower hangs down. Several grasslike leaves. Plant 4-12".

Petals and sepals are all alike; yellow to orange-brown; red when aging. Plains-Montane. Northern Colo. north. *Fritillary pudica,* Lily Family.

BIGELOW SENECIO
(p. 194)

Fleshy, top-shaped head 3/4" long,* of disk flowers only; hangs down, appears closed. A few straggling bracts at base. Alternate leaves, toothed.

Pale yellow disk flowers; bracts may be yellow to purplish or brownish-green. A few slender, 1/2" bracts in an outer row generally spread out like spider legs. Leaves, 4-8" long, are lance-shaped and pointed. Plant, 1-3' tall, is stout, unbranched, and hairy. Montane-Subalpine. Colo., New Mex. and Ariz. *Senecio bigelovi,* Composite Family.

A similar but daintier species is *NODDING SENECIO with heads about half as large. It is nodding, rayless, cylindric and not fleshy. Foothills-Montane. *Senecio pudicus.*

PARRY ARNICA or Rayless Arnica—is much like Bigelow Senecio only—the buds nod but the mature flowers usually do not; there are no straggly bracts; and the leaves are opposite. Flowers are never purplish and plant is 1 to 1-1/2'. Colo. north. *Arnica parryi,* Composite Family.

192

BROOMRAPE
(See Red/Misc.)

> 2-lipped tube flower. Leaves like scales. No green on plant. 6″ or less.

BLACK MEDIC

> Heads of extremely tiny, crowded pea flowers. Clover-like leaves. <u>Prostrate plant</u>.

Stems, 1-2′ long, are woody, square and grooved. Common lawn weed. Plains-Foothills. *Medicago lupulina,* Pea Family.

Snow-lily

Yellow Lady-slipper

Golden Smoke

Bigelow Senecio

Leafy Spurge
(p. 208)

One-sided Pyrola
(p. 203)

Poison Ivy
(p. 202)

Green Bog-orchid
(p. 201)

Curly Dock
(p. 200)

Sibbaldia
(p. 211)

Stinging Nettle
(p. 202)

Pine-drops
(p. 203)

SMOOTH SUMAC
or Rocky Mountain
Sumac
(p. 198)

1/4″ flowers in dense pointed heads 4-8″ long. Variable color. Large, alternate leaves have 9 to 21 narrow, toothed leaflets green above, pale below. On sandy banks and road-sides.

Flowers are whitish, creamy, or greenish-yellow. The 2-5″ leaflets turn brilliant shades of red in autumn. Shrub, 2-6′ tall, usually grows in large clumps and the stout stems have leafy twigs, often reddish. Small, red, velvety fruits are in pyramid clusters. Foothills. *Rhus glabra,* Sumac Family.

NOTES. This shrub contains tannic acid, used in tanning leather. The Indians made a dye from the roots.

**MOUNTAIN
  MAHOGANY**
or Feather Bush
(p. 198)

No petals. Flowers are red-tipped tubes 1/4″ long. Clusters of 1″, ovate, deeply veined leaves. Gray bark. Seeds have feathery, twisted tails. Sunny hills.

Flowers bloom early and are not noticeable. The feathery seed plumes, however, with fuzzy, twisted tails 2-4″ long, are very attractive from late summer into winter. Alternate clusters of 2 to 5 toothed leaves are shiny green above and pale below. Shrub, 3-6′ (rarely 9′) is irregularly shaped, and very common on rocky slopes. Foothills-Montane. It is called "mahogany" because the wood is so hard. *Cercocarpus montanus,* Rose Family.

BIG SAGEBRUSH
(p. 198)

1/4″ inconspicuous flowers. Narrow leaves 3-toothed at tip. Rigid stems. Gray-green shrub with typical sage odor. Dry soil.

The pollen of the many silvery-green or yellowish flowers is one cause of hay fever. Leaves are wedge-shaped and bluish-silvery. Shrub is 6″ to 12′ tall (commonly 1 to 4′), and much branched, with shreddy bark. Sagebrush grows in dry soil, covering large areas, sometimes many square miles. Plains-Subalpine. The sage odor is especially strong after a rain. *Artemisia tridentata,* Composite Family.

NOTES. The presence of sagebrush indicates fertile soil. Early settlers judged the quality of the soil by the height of the sagebrush.
    Although not their favorite food, it saves many animals from starvation in late winter when other food is scarce—deer, elk,

moose, grouse, rabbits, sheep and cattle. It also provides den sites and cover for small animals.

Indians obtained a yellow dye from sagebrush.

BUFFALO-BERRY	No petals. Inconspicuous flowers; bloom before leaves open. Leaves opposite, entire; have rusty or silvery scales. Red or orange berries.

1. **BITTER BUFFALO-BERRY**—Leaves ovate, green above, have rusty scales below. Shrub 3-9'. No thorns. Berries are bitter. Montane-Subalpine. *Shepherdia canadensis,* Oleaster Family.
2. **SILVER BUFFALO-BERRY**—Leaves oblong and silvery-scurfy both sides. Shrub (or tree) 6-20'. Has thorns. Berries are edible and Indians and pioneers mixed them with stew and meat dishes, hence the name, "buffalo-berry." Plains-Montane. *Shepherdia argentea.* These shrubs are related to the widely cultivated Russian Olive tree.

Smooth Sumac   **Mountain Mahogany**   **Big Sagebrush**

FALSE HELLEBORE
or Corn-lily
(p. 205)

> 6 lobes. Many clusters of greenish-white star flowers on spreading branches. Leaves large, wide and plaited. Tall coarse stem. Marshy ground.

Flower branches usually become shorter towards the top of the spike, thus forming a large, roughly pyramidal inflorescence. Flowers, 1/2 to 1″ are green at the base and white towards the tips of the 6 petals and sepals. Leaves are 4-12″ long and 3-8″ wide. They are sessile, strongly parallel-veined, clasp the stem, and are plaited. The plaits are gathered into the base of the leaf, but the leaf tips are pointed. The stout stem, 2-8′ tall, usually grows in dense clumps, and is more common on the Western Slope. Montane-Subalpine. The red berries are the size of small peas. *Veratrum tenuipetalum,* Lily Family.

NOTE. Although False Hellebore is poisonous, it is used in medicine for the heart and for high blood pressure. Indians used it for this and probably introduced it to pioneers.

GREEN GENTIAN
or Monument Plant
(p. 205)

> 4 petals. Pale green saucer flowers 1-2″ wide, along spikes; pointed petals have purplish markings and fringed glands. Large leaves in whorls. Plant 6″ to 6′ tall.

If viewed from a distance, the greenish-white flowers are not particularly pretty but when examined closely are very attractive. 4 slender, pointed sepals alternate with the petals. Leaves are long, 1 to 2-1/2″ wide, entire, and sometimes tinged with purple. The first summer there is only a basal rosette of long leaves. The second year, the flowering stalk develops and the basal leaves wither. The whorled stem leaves decrease in size towards top of plant. The single, stout, pale green stem is often seen in large colonies. Foothills-Montane. *Frasera speciosa,* Gentian Family.

GIANT LOUSEWORT
or Grays Lousewort,
or Indian Warrior
(p. 205)

> Greenish or dingy-yellow 2-lipped flowers, usually streaked with red. Upper lip compressed on sides and strongly arched, almost touching lower lip. Fernlike leaves up to 1′ long.

Flowers about 1-1/4″ long. Plant usually has a single, erect, stout stem 1-4′ tall. Montane-Subalpine. Found in moist woods; Wyo. and Utah south. *Pedicularis grayi,* Figwort Family.

DOCK

(p. 206)
(color plate p. 196)

> Tiny flowers <u>look like green seeds,</u> in dense, cylindrical clusters. Later, the brownish <u>fruit looks like coffee grains.</u> <u>Leaves alternate.</u> Stout, erect stem. 3 common species are:

1. **CURLY DOCK**—When fully ripe, the fruit of all dock species has tiny wings. Leaves are dark green, oblong to lance-shaped, 4-12″ long, pointed, and have <u>wavy or curly margins.</u> The sturdy stem is 1-4′ tall, is grooved, and has a papery sheath at the leaf nodes. This common plant prefers valleys and cultivated ground. Plains-Foothills. *Rumex crispus,* Buckwheat Family.

2. **WILLOW DOCK**—Flowers and fruits like those of Curly Dock. Leaves are pale green, narrow, entire, and pointed at both ends. Plant has <u>axillary</u> shoots, i.e., stems and leaves growing out of other leaf axils. Common along roadsides. Foothills-Montane. *Rumex triangulivalis.*

   NOTE. The docks bloom chiefly during June or July but are more conspicuous later because the reddish-brown fruits are more noticeable than the little, green flowers.

3. **WESTERN DOCK**—Flowers and fruits like those of Curly Dock. Leaves are 4-16″ long on petioles equally long. They are entire and parallel-veined with veins at an angle to the midrib. This sturdy plant, 2-6′ tall, grows along streams and in damp places. Montane-Subalpine. *Rumex occidentalis.*

TASSELFLOWER

> Heads of greenish-yellow <u>disk flowers hang down.</u> Leaves alternate, toothed, <u>triangular.</u> Plant 1-3′.

Heads of greenish-cream to yellowish flowers hang from ends of stalks. Branched plant, in rocky canyons. Plains-Montane. *Brickellia grandiflora,* Composite Family.

SPOTTED CORAL-ROOT

(p. 206)

> 1/2″ brownish-purple orchid flowers (see Key Terms). 6 lobes, including the large, <u>white, purple-spotted lip.</u> *A tooth on each side of lip. <u>No leaves.</u> <u>No green on plant.</u>

*The lip of an orchid is its lowest petal which is usually also the largest and most decorative of the 6 petals and sepals. It serves as a landing pad for the insects needed to pollinate the orchids.

A few membranous tissues sheathe the stem and match it in color. In spring, the plant sends up slender, asparagus-like spears that are usually pinkish-brown or yellowish-brown; sometimes one will be white. This is a saprophyte; that is, it lives on dead organic matter such as rotten wood under the dry needles in pine forests. Foothills-Timberline. Plant, 6-20″ tall, requires less moisture than other orchids, and its little, purple-spotted flowers look as though they are laughing. *Corallorhiza maculata,* Orchid Family.

YELLOW STEM CORAL-ROOT	Like the preceding except that the white lip has no spots, and the stem is slender and yellow or greenish-yellow.

In damp forests. Montane-Subalpine. Colo. north. *Corallorhiza trifida.* The roots of these plants are branched and interwoven like coral, hence the name.

ORCHID FAMILY

This is the largest of all plant families, with over 20,000 different species, ranging from tiny ones that will fit in a thimble to tree-like vines 50 feet long. The great majority of orchids grow in tropical and sub-tropical lands. Only a few have been able to survive in colder climates like Alaska, northern Europe, and Asia. Most of Colorado's 2 dozen species are small and easily overlooked. Yellow Lady-slipper and Fairy-slipper are beautiful exceptions, but both are becoming very rare in the Rockies.

Orchids are not parasites as was once commonly believed. Tropical orchids use trees for support only and derive food from the rain, air and dust. Orchids in colder regions, like the Rocky Mtns., live largely on disintegrating beds of litter, lichens, mosses and wood. (The coral-roots, lacking chlorophyll, may—perhaps—be partially parasitic.)

One interesting genus is the Vanilla Orchid from which the flavoring extract is obtained. It grows in subtropical countries, including Madagascar and Mexico, and a few species are raised in southern Florida.

GREEN BOG-ORCHIDS *(p. 206)* *(color plate p. 195)*	1/4″ greenish orchid-flowers along top part of a single, erect stem. Tiny spur at base of lip. Long, entire leaves. Wet places.

The greenish-white flowers may be touched with purple. Plant, 4-12″, grows in wet soil. Montane-Subalpine. Although common, it is easily overlooked because the greenish flowers blend with the surrounding grass and sedges. *Habenaria hyperborea, saccata,* and others, Orchid Family.

<table>
<tr><td>

POISON IVY
or Poison Oak
(p. 206)
(color plate p. 195)

</td><td>

Do Not Touch. See Notes.
Axillary clusters of yellowish-white flowers 1/4" wide. Leaves alternate on long petioles; have <u>3 broad, pointed, shiny leaflets</u>, 1-8" long; <u>often drooping</u>.

</td></tr>
</table>

The bright green, ovate leaflets may be entire or toothed, and the end leaflet has the longest petiole. In autumn, the leaves turn beautiful shades of red and orange. Plant may be either a single, woody stem 6-24" tall, or a woody vine climbing trees. Fruits are shiny, yellowish-white berries. Plains-Foothills. *Toxicodendron radicans* or *Rhus radicans,* Sumac Family.

NOTES. Poison Ivy—also called Poison Oak—is found throughout the United States, and in some areas is much larger than in the Rockies. It contains the poisonous oil, urushiol, in all parts of the plant but particularly the leaves. If brought into contact with the skin, this poison may cause inflammation, swelling and blisters. People vary greatly in their susceptibility to poison ivy, some developing very painful cases of poisoning, others appearing to be immune. This immunity, however, has been known to cease without warning. Being wet or sweaty at time of contact makes one more susceptible. Smoke from burning poison ivy is most injurious to the eyes.

Thorough washing in strong soap will usually remove the poison if done immediately after touching the plant. Even clear water helps. Prompt application of household ammonia stops the itching.

Urushiol is an important component of Japanese and Chinese lacquers. Poison Ivy is related to the Cashew Nut which is contained in a highly poisonous shell but is, of course, deliciously edible after being roasted and shelled.

<table>
<tr><td>

STINGING NETTLE
or Common Nettle
(p. 206)
(color plate p. 196)

</td><td>

Do Not Touch. See Note.
Small <u>axillary clusters</u> of tiny, greenish flowers; <u>no petals</u>. Leaves opposite, sharply toothed, crinkled, and paler below. <u>Have stipules</u>.*
Square stems.

</td></tr>
</table>

Leaves are dark green, narrow-ovate, and have a very uneven surface. *Stipules are leaf-like appendages at the base of the petiole. The straight stems, 1-6' tall, generally grow in moist locations or on waste ground, often in clumps. Plains-Montane. *Urtica dioica ssp. gracilis,* Nettle Family.

NOTE. Both leaves and stems have hairs containing an acid that causes some people pain and inflammation on contact.

PINE-DROPS *(p. 206)* *(color plate p. 195)*	5 petals. 1/4″ bell- or urn-shaped flowers hang along stout stem. No green on plant. Instead, the narrow, basal leaves are pinkish-brown.

No Green Leaves. They are reduced to scales or small leaves the same color as the stem. The stems, often 2 or more, are 10-36″ high, unbranched, and sticky-hairy. In spring, they are usually pinkish but soon turn purplish-brown. Found in dry, evergreen forests. Foothills-Montane. Alaska to Mexico. *Pterospora andromedea,* Heath Family.

NOTE. Pine-drops contains no chlorophyll. It is a saprophyte; that is, it obtains its food from decaying plant material such as rotting wood.

ONE-SIDED PYROLA or Sidebells Wintergreen *(p. 206)* *(Color plate p. 195)*	5 fleshy petals. Small, roundish, nodding, greenish-white flowers with large, protruding style; hang along one side of stem. Ovate leaves. Plant 3-8″ in damp forests.

Buds resemble 1/4″ greenish cherries. Flower stem is often curved. Leaves are evergreen and mostly in a basal rosette, with a few on the stem. Plant grows in shady forests. Foothills-Subalpine. Although sometimes called wintergreen, it does not have the flavor of the true wintergreen. *Pyrola secunda,* Heath Family.

LESSER WINTERGREEN—is similar to the preceding but the flowers, either white or pink, are on all sides of the stem, and all leaves are basal. Montane-Alpine. *Pyrola minor.*

MEADOW-RUE *(p. 206)* *(color plate p. 196)*	Tiny, drooping, greenish flowers look like tassels. Delicate leaves have rounded, divided leaflets. Plant 1-2′*.

Flowers are greenish or yellowish-green tassels; when aging, they turn brownish. No petals or rays but the small sepals look like petals. Leaves are bluish-green or yellowish-green. Plant · is branched and has considerable foliage. Found in moist meadows and aspen groves. Foothills-Subalpine. Wyo. south. *Thalictrum fendleri* and *sparsiflorum*. Buttercup Family.

*ALPINE MEADOW-RUE—is very similar but it is 2-12″ tall, and the leaf edges tend to turn down. Subalpine-Alpine. *Thalictrum alpinum.*

ALUMROOT *(p. 206)*	Tiny, greenish-yellowish flowers along leafless stem 4-24″ tall. All leaves basal, lobed, and green. In rocky places. 2 common species are:

OTHER COLORS STALK

1. **COMMON ALUMROOT**—Flowers are usually in small, separated clusters along top part of stem. Leaves, long-petioled, 1-2″ wide, have 5 to 9 lobes with rounded teeth. Plant 8-24″ tall, grows in rocky places, often in shade. Plains-Foothills. *Heuchera parvifolia,* Saxifrage Family. Colorado has a shorter alpine variety—H. parvifolia var. nivalis—4-8″.
2. **BRACTED ALUMROOT**—Flowers hang along one side of stem. Stamens protrude. Leaf lobes are sharply toothed. Some rust-colored leaves may hang on throughout the winter. Plant, 4-8″, often forms tufts on rock ledges and crevices. Foothills. Colo. and Wyo. *Heuchera bracteata.*

FRINGED MOUNTAIN SAGE *(p. 206)*	Tiny rounded heads of disk flowers only; nod along small branches on a 1′ stem rising above a low, dense tuft or puff of soft, silvery, fringy leaves.

Yellowish heads are interspersed with tiny, cut leaves. Although a late bloomer, the plant starts up early in spring and the silvery tufts are widespread on dry, gravelly hillsides throughout the growing season. It is 2-6″ tall but the flower stems in Aug. and Sep. may be 10-16″. Foothills-Subalpine. Plant has a sage odor and is related to the common sagebrush. *Artemisia frigida,* Composite Family.

NOTE. Pioneers made a bitter tea from this plant, which they used as a tonic, and as a remedy for mountain fever (typhoid fever).

ALPINE SAGE or Alpine Mountain Sage	Tiny heads of disk flowers only. Bract edges dark brown or purple. Silvery leaves much divided. Chiefly alpine.

Flowers greenish—or brownish-yellow; may or may not nod. Silky-hairy plant 1′ or less; may have reddish stems. *Artemisia scopulorum* and others, Composite Family.

VIRGINIA CREEPER or Woodbine	5 greenish petals. Leaves alternate; 5 (or 7) palmate leaflets green both sides; large teeth. Climbing vine with tendrils.

Pointed leaflets turn red in fall. Black berries on red stems. Found in woods and on river banks. Plains-Foothills. Wyo. to New Mex. and Ariz. *Parthenocissus vitacea,* Grape Family.

ALPINE SORREL (See Red/Stalk)	Tiny green or reddish flowers look like seeds, are very thick. No petals or rays. Leaves kidney-shaped (or round). Plant 3-12".

BISHOPS CAP or Miterwort *(p. 206)*	5 tiny, feathery petals are cut along their sides. Greenish flowers along a 4-12" stem. All leaves basal and scalloped. Wet soil.

Petals are attached to a tiny, green calyx cup which remains on the stem after petals have withered. Leaves, nearly round, are 1-2" across. The single stem grows in wet places in shady forests. Montane-Subalpine. Colo. to Alaska. *Mitella pentandra,* Saxifrage Family.

OTHER COLORS STALK

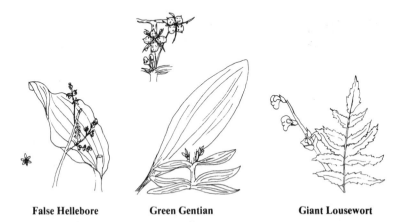

False Hellebore   Green Gentian   Giant Lousewort

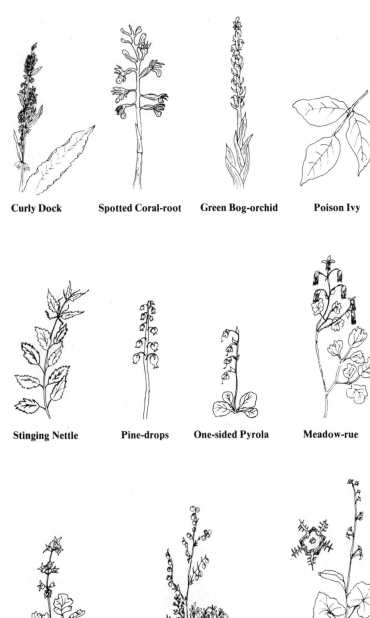

Curly Dock   **Spotted Coral-root**   **Green Bog-orchid**   **Poison Ivy**

Stinging Nettle   **Pine-drops**   **One-sided Pyrola**   **Meadow-rue**

Common Alumroot   **Fringed Mountain Sage**   **Bishops Cap**

WOOLLY THISTLE or Frosty Ball or Hooker Thistle *(p. 210)*	Dense, silvery, cobwebby, ball-like flower cluster, 1-1/2 to 3″. Looks soft-woolly but the narrow leaves circling the ball are very spiny. Usually nodding. Usually alpine.

The cluster of pale or creamy-white heads is nearly hidden by spiny leaves and long, dense, cobwebby hair. The whole "woolly" top generally bends over. Plant is 6-24″ high. Colo. and Utah north. *Cirsium scopulorum,* or *hookerianum,* Composite Family.

AMERICAN THISTLE	1-1/2″ "brushy" heads of disk flowers only, usually grayish-white. Prickly leaves green above and white below; are decurrent.* Spiny plant 1-3′.

All thistles are composed of disk flowers only; unusually long ones that are split into narrow divisions, giving the heads a fluffy appearance. American Thistle flowers may be white, pinkish or yellowish but not purple. They are usually grayish-white. The bracts are loose, and fringed at the tips with the fringe pointing upwards. Bracts have no ridges down the middle but each has a short, weak spine. Heads are nearly sessile at ends of branches. *Leaves are decurrent, that is, leaf tissue extends down the plant stem 1-3″ below the base of the leaf. Found in ravines, often in colonies. Montane-Subalpine. Wyo., Utah and Colo. *Cirsium centaureae,* Composite Family.

NOTE. Wavy-leaf Thistle (in Red/Heads) is sometimes grayish-white but its flowers are on long stems, the bracts are firmly overlapped, and its leaf bases clasp the plant stem.

Elk Thistle (in White/Heads) may be grayish but its flowers are sessile in the leaf axils and at top of main stem, and a few leaves often extend up to or above the top flower. Leaves may or may not be decurrent, the plant stem is almost as thick at the top as at the base, and it prefers damp places.

This book includes 8 of over 20 species of thistle found in this area.

YELLOW PAINTBRUSH (See Yellow/Head)	Yellow-green to whitish cluster 1-1/2 to 3″ long of 1 to 1-1/2″ vertically overlapping "petals." Small green, pointed tips may protrude from these "petals."

GRAYS ANGELICA

(p. 210)

> Umbels 1-2″ wide, of tiny flowers variable in color. Divided leaves with wide bases clasping stems. <u>Ovate</u> <u>leaflets</u>. Sturdy stems 6-24″.

Flowers are in double umbels, as in almost all of the carrot family. In this species, the large umbel is usually rather flat, the small ones are globe-shaped. Flowers are greenish to purplish-brown. Fruits are brown. Usually one stout, thick stem; often found among rocks. Montane-Alpine. *Angelica grayi,* Carrot Family.

SPURGE

(p. 210)
(color plate p. 195)

> 1-3″ umbels of tiny flowers with wide, green or yellowish, petal-like <u>bracts</u>.* Leaves alternate and <u>whorl-ed</u>; entire. 2 species follow.

*On each flower stem is an umbel with 3 to 6 small pedicels; each pedicel bears a pair of wide green (or yellow) bracts from which rises a smaller umbel with 2 more bracts. At the top umbel, the bracts surround the 1/16″ flowers and 4 tiny glands, best seen with a lens. There are no petals or sepals so the bracts look more like a blossom than do the flowers themselves. The leaves just below the flowers are whorled.

1. **ROCKY MOUNTAIN SPURGE**—Flowers are <u>all green;</u> leaves are mostly ovate, and fleshy (plump); and plant <u>is entirely green</u>, except for—sometimes—a reddish base. The <u>several</u> stout, non-hairy <u>stems, 4-12″ tall</u>, have milky juice. Found on sunny, rocky slopes. Plains-Montane. *Euphorbia robusta,* Spurge Family.

2. **LEAFY SPURGE**—The <u>flower bracts and upper leaves</u>—linear to oblong—<u>are yellowish-green</u>. Plant <u>usually has a single stem</u> <u>1-3′ tall</u>, growing in moist fields and on roadsides. Both species are poisonous, and Leafy Spurge is a troublesome weed. *Euphorbia esula.*

NOTE. The Christmas flower, poinsettia, and the castor-oil bean belong to the spurge family and these, too, are poisonous. Tapioca is made from another poisonous member of the family, the cassava plant. However after the poison has been removed, both tapioca and a very nutritious flour can be made from cassava. This flour is a staple food in South America.

208

ARCTIC GENTIAN *(p. 210)*	Usually 5 petals. Cluster of cup-shaped flowers 1-1/2″ deep; dotted inside and streaked outside with purple and blue; salmon-pink stamens. Leaves both opposite and basal. Plant 2-8″ tall.

Generally 2 or 3 greenish-white or yellowish flowers in a cluster. This is a pleated gentian; i.e., it has a pleat or fold of tissue between the petals. The buds and closed flowers appear dark. Leaves, 1-4″, are linear to oblong. The one to several stems each bear a flower cluster. Subalpine-Alpine. This is the last flower to bloom in the alpine zone. *Gentiana algida* or *romanzovii,* Gentian Family.

PARRY THISTLE (See Yellow/Head)	1″ greenish-yellow flower puffs in a nest of spiny, spider-webby bracts. Narrow, prickly leaves. Thick, grooved, spiny stem 1-4′ tall.

PARRY ARNICA or **NODDING SENECIO** (See Yellow/Misc.)	Fleshy flower head 1/2″ long, hangs down, appears closed. Yellow to greenish-yellow to purplish-brown. All disk flowers; no rays or petals. Stout, unbranched plant 1-3′ tall.

DUSTY MAIDEN or Pincushion Plant *(p. 210)*	1/2″ erect heads of disk flowers only, whitish or pink to gray. Stamens protrude. Leaves grayish, thick-textured, and much cut. Sturdy, erect stems 8-14″ tall. Plant looks dusty.

Flowers are white or pinkish but the dark stamens make them appear gray or flesh color. Narrow, even bracts form a 1/2″ cylindrical base, somewhat ribbed, and the reddish-brown stamens stick out like tiny pins in a cushion. Leaves are alternate and leathery. They are 2 or 3 times divided with the last segments not especially narrow. There is a basal rosette of leaves—sometimes withered, but still present. Plant has one to several leafy stems, and grows on dry, rocky places. Foothills-Montane. *Chaenactis douglasii,* Composite Family.

PALE COMANDRA or Bastard Toadflax	5 (or 4) "petals". 1/4″ star flowers; white, pink, or green. All leaves alternate, entire, sessile, oblong, bluish. Plant 6-12″.

Crowded flower cluster. Leaves are non-hairy. This plant is

parasitic, and is common in spring. Plains-Foothills. *Comandra umbellata* or *pallida,* Sandalwood Family.

SALT AND PEPPER or Biscuitroot *(p. 210)*	Grayish umbel of 1/8″ flowers. Gray-green leaves are much cut. Plant low, delicate, hairy, and inconspicuous.

The tiny petals are white or pale pink but purplish bracts and projecting black-headed stamens give the flowers a speckled, gray appearance. This little flower, so easily overlooked, is one of the first to appear in spring. Leaves are flat on the ground at first but as the stem grows taller, it lifts them. When the plant begins blooming, the stems are about 1″ high; later they reach a height of 4-16″. Found on dry places. Plains-Foothills. Colo. to Mont. *Lomatium orientale* or *Cogswellia orientalis,* Carrot Family.

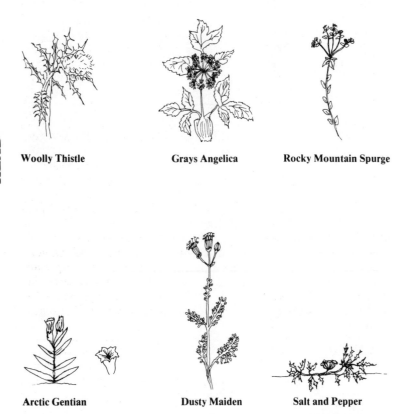

Woolly Thistle   Grays Angelica   Rocky Mountain Spurge

Arctic Gentian   Dusty Maiden   Salt and Pepper

CANDLE ANEMONE

3/4" flower with greenish-white "petals"; on a long, naked stem. Leaves basal with a whorl of leaf-like bracts low on the 1-2' stem. Cylindrical, woolly seed head.

All leaves and bracts much divided, and have petioles. The circle of bracts was wrapped around the flower bud before it pushed upward and opened. Foothills-Montane. *Anemone cylindrica,* Buttercup Family.

SIBBALDIA

(color plate p. 196)

Flat flowers about 1/6". 5 tiny, pale yellow, separated petals framed by green sepals. Tiny clover-like leaves. Plant usually flat on ground. Chiefly alpine.

The yellow petals are shorter than the green sepals so green color predominates even when the plant is blooming. Leaves are blue-green with 3 short, toothed leaflets. Plant is a low cushion 1-2" high—rarely to 6", and it is easily overlooked. Found on rocky or gravelly slopes throughout the northern hemisphere in alpine locations. *Sibbaldia procumbens,* Rose Family.

LEAVES

A LEAF consists of:

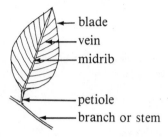

1. a blade
2. a petiole or stem (usually)
   If there is no petiole, the leaf is called <u>sessile.</u>

   A leaf blade has a midrib and veins.

Sometimes at the base of a leaf there many be a small bud. And sometimes at the base there may be a pair of small leaflike (or papery) appendages called <u>stipules.</u>

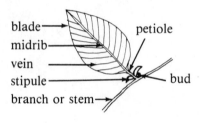

A. Simple Leaf: the blade is in a single part. Blade shapes vary.

Example:

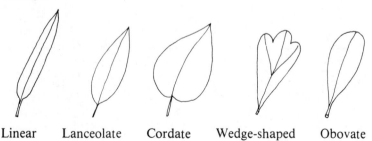

Linear   Lanceolate   Cordate   Wedge-shaped   Obovate

B. Compound Leaf: the blade is divided into several parts called leaflets. The leaflets may be arranged in two different ways:

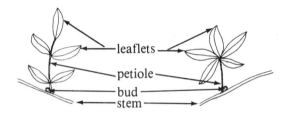

leaflets

petiole

bud

stem

1. Pinnately compound—leaflets along each side of a common petiole.

2. Palmately compound—leaflets grouped at tip of petiole.

LEAF or LEAFLET?

This may sometimes be confusing at first. Size is no indication because both leaves and leaflets in this region range from less than 1/4″ to more than 1′.

1. Look for a bud in the axil. There is <u>never</u> any bud at the base of a leaflet. There is <u>always</u> a bud at the base of a compound leaf. There is usually a bud where a simple leaf joins the branch but not always. If there are no buds anywhere, then all the blades are leaves, not leaflets. These little buds are called axillary buds; they are not flower buds.

2. The color and texture of a leaf petiole is nearly always somewhat different from that of the branch or stem to which it is attached, but a leaflet stalk (if there is one) is very similar in color and texture to that of the main petiole of the compound leaf to which it belongs.

LEAF MARGINS—and also leaflet margins—may be:

1. Entire,
2. Toothed,
3. Lobed.

1. Entire— even, having no teeth, lobes nor divisions.

2. Toothed.

213

3. Lobed—a leaf may be:

  A. Pinnately lobed
      or
  B. Palmately lobed

and these lobes may be entire, or toothed, or themselves lobed.

Simple leaf—
Pinnately lobed.

Simple leaf—
Palmately lobed
and toothed.

LEAF ARRANGEMENTS

Leaves may be arranged along the stem in 3 different ways:

Alternate
(most common)

Opposite

Whorled
3 or more leaves
at one node
(least common)

IMPORTANT. A knowledge of leaf margins and arrangements is a
great help in identifying flowers.

PARTS OF A TYPICAL FLOWER

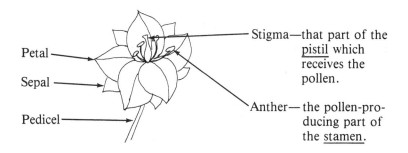

Petal

Sepal

Pedicel

Stigma—that part of the <u>pistil</u> which receives the pollen.

Anther— the pollen-pro-ducing part of the <u>stamen</u>.

CROSS-SECTION OF A TYPICAL FLOWER

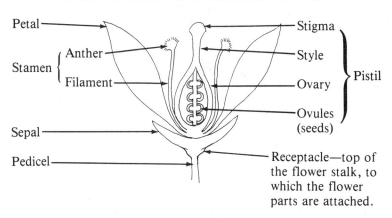

Petal

Stamen { Anther

Filament

Sepal

Pedicel

Stigma

Style

Ovary

Ovules (seeds)

Pistil

Receptacle—top of the flower stalk, to which the flower parts are attached.

Ovary is <u>superior</u> if stamens, petals, and <u>sepals</u> are attached to the receptacle <u>below</u> it;

Ovary is <u>inferior</u> if they are attached <u>above</u>.

COMPOSITE FLOWER

Ray flower⟶   ⟵Disk Flowers

CROSS-SECTION OF COMPOSITE FLOWER

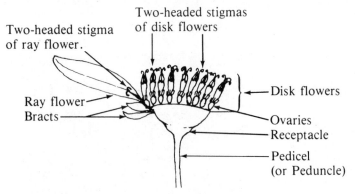

Two-headed stigma
of ray flower.

Two-headed stigmas
of disk flowers

Ray flower⟶
Bracts⟶

Disk flowers

Ovaries
Receptacle

Pedicel
(or Peduncle)

In some species, only the disk flowers produce seeds. In others, only the ray flowers are fertile. But in most cases both ray and disk flowers produce seeds.

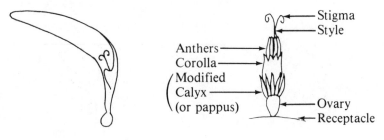

Anthers⟶
Corolla⟶
Modified
Calyx⟶
(or pappus)

Stigma
Style

Ovary
Receptacle

Detail of Ray Flower   Detail of Disk Flower

At one stage, the ring of anthers is pushed up as high or higher than the stigmas.

216

GLOSSARY

Anther—that part of the stamen which produces the pollen.

Ascending—said of stems nearly prostrate near the base but curving up towards the tip.

Banner—the broad, erect, upper petal of pea flowers.

Bract—a much reduced—and usually much modified—leaf with no petiole; generally close below a flower or a flower cluster.

Many flower species may have one to several bracts but "Daisy" (composite) flowers always have a set. These bracts could be mistaken for sepals. However in the composite flowers, the true sepals are small and modified, and can best be seen with a lens. The bracts, on the other hand, are easily seen and they usually form a sort of cup—called an involucre—around the base of the flower. There may be 1 to 3 or more rows of bracts and these provide one good way of identifying members of the Composite Family.

Catkin—a spike of inconspicuous flowers; no petals or rays, just scaly bracts; as on willow trees and birches. A catkin may or may not hang down, and some are short. Pussy willows are willows having large, cylindrical, silky catkins that come before the leaves open.

Composite—collection of many flowers in a single, tightly-packed head. Although each blossom looks like a single flower, it is actually composed of many flowers crowded together in one head. The head looks like a blossom; the individual flowers do not.

The Composite (kahm PAHZ it) Family has around 500 species in this area and is divided into 3 groups.

Group 1. Has two kinds of flowers:
A. Tiny, slender, tubular flowers, called disks, tightly packed in the center of the head—like a button.
B. Petal-like flowers, called rays, varying in size and number, surrounding the button like a circle of fringe.

This is much the largest group of composites, and includes daisies, sunflowers, and many others.

The "button" center of these composites is not always entirely even, because at one stage the tiny stigmas (which receive the pollen and are usually two-branched) may be pushed up 1/16"; at another time, the little anthers (which produce the pollen) may be raised slightly.

Group 2. Has disk flowers only, like thistles and pussytoes. In this book, flowers of the thistle type have been placed in "Heads."

Group 3. Has ray flowers only, like dandelions and salsify. These are listed under "Saucers."

Compound—made up of two to many similar parts, as a compound leaf.

Daisy—Aster distinctions—Daisies are frequently hard to distinguish from Asters. The following may help:

DAISIES	ASTERS
Rays are usually comparatively narrow.	Rays are rather wide—1/8″ or more.
Rays are very numerous, about 30 to 175.	Rays are comparatively few, usually less than 30.
Bloom mostly in spring and early summer.	Bloom in late summer and fall.

The surest distinction lies in the bracts:

Daisy bracts (on back of flower head) are of nearly equal length and they form 1 or 2 rows.

Aster bracts are almost always in 3 or more rows; the bracts are of varying lengths and they overlap each other unevenly like shingles on a roof.

Townsendia bracts, also, overlap unevenly.

Decurrent—said of the base of a leaf that continues down the stem one to several inches below the axil.

Dioecious—said of plants having pistillate flowers (with pistils only) on one individual, and staminate flowers (with stamens only) on another plant of the same species.

Filament—the thread-like stalk supporting an anther.

Fleshy—plump, having body or substance, not thin, dry, or membranous. Fleshy leaves are nearly circular in cross-section, instead of flat.

Floret—a small flower, especially one in a dense cluster.

Head—a compact cluster of numerous, small flowers.

Inflorescence—the flowering part of a plant and its arrangement.

Involucre—a whorl or set of bracts around a flower or a flower head; usually referring to a composite flower. The florets of composite flowers are packed tightly together and surrounded at the base by several to many bracts, called collectively, the involucre. The involucre at the base of a composite flower corresponds roughly to the calyx of sepals on a typical flower, except that the involucre usually has more bracts and they are generally arranged in overlapping rows.

Irregular—said of a flower in which the petals are not all alike.

Leaf—a simple leaf is either not divided at all or is divided not more than half-way to its midrib, into parts called lobes.

a compound leaf is completely separated into 2 to many similar parts called leaflets.

Lobe—a part of a leaf blade. The term is often used loosely, but technically it refers to a part of a leaf that is divided not more than half-way to the midrib, and is rounded both between the lobes and at their ends.

Lobe is also sometimes applied to a petal, as being a part of a flower.

Monoecious—said of plants having both pistils and stamens on the same plant.

Node—the point on a stem from which one or more leaves arise.

Ovary—the part of the pistil that contains the ovules. It ripens into the seed pod.

Ovule—tiny body in the ovary which becomes a seed after fertilization.

Pappus—In the composite family, the minute calyx of each tiny flower is modified into hairs, awns, or bristles, called pappus. These are inside the circle of bracts or involucre, and when the seeds are ripe this pappus helps distribute them. The hairs may be blown far away by the wind—as the "parachute" of a dandelion seed; the awns or scales may be blown along the ground, and the bristles may hook on to animal fur or people's clothing.

Phyllary—one of the bracts in the involucre of a composite flower.

Pollen—the fertilizing grains of a plant. Pollen must reach the stigma and pass down to the ovary if fertilization is to take place.

Pollination—the transfer of pollen from a stamen to a stigma. It may be brought about by the wind, water, animals, birds, insects, etc., but the most important agents are wind and insects. There are two kinds of pollination. Self-pollination is the transfer of pollen from a stamen to the stigma of the same flower or to the stigma of another flower on the same plant. Cross-pollination is the transfer of pollen to a stigma on another plant.

Prostrate—lying flat on the ground.

Runner—slender stem lying along ground and sending down roots at intervals; also sending up leaves.

Scape—a leafless flowering stalk.

Sheathe—to wrap around, enclose; as the lower part of a grass leaf sheathes the stem.

Simple—said of a leaf if its blade consists of a single piece.

Stigma—the part of the pistil which receives the pollen.

Stipules—appendages, usually leaf-like, sometimes found at the base of the petiole of a leaf in certain plants. May occur singly or in pairs.

Style—the part of the pistil which connects the stigma with the ovary. It is sometimes absent; the stigma being sessile.

PLANT ZONES

Different ecologists list varying altitudes and give different names to the plant zones. The following table is the simplest and is fairly accurate in Colorado but not in northern or southern Rockies. Timberline, for instance, is higher in New Mexico than in Colorado but is considerably lower in Montana.

COLORADO PLANT ZONES

Plains	Zone approximately	4,000 to 6,000 feet elevation	
Foothills	" "	6,000 to 8,000 " "	
Montane	" "	8,000 to 10,000 " "	
Subalpine	" "	10,000 to 11,500 " "	
		(or around timberline)	
Alpine	" "	above timberline.	

One way to recognize zones is by the growth. Plains are grasslands. Foothills have shrubs.

The Montane zone is forested. In northern Montana, this zone begins close to the plains, at about 4,000 feet. In New Mexico and Arizona, it is almost entirely above 8,000 feet.

Subalpine is distinguished by large tracts of unbroken conifer forests, interrupted only by creeks, rocky outcrops, and a few grassy meadows.

Alpine is, of course, treeless with rocky grassland called tundra.

Along the Subalpine-Alpine boundary is often a timberline forest called "Elfinwood." Weighed down and bent in winter by heavy snows, swept by strong western winds, with needles shortened to conserve moisture, and growing in scanty, poor-quality soil, the trees form twisted, fascinating, grotesque shapes. Some are so short that they merely spread out along the ground.

PETALS vs RAYS

They may look alike but they perform different functions.

PETALS aid in the pollination of plants. Without pollination, no seeds would ever develop. In some species, pollination is done by wind but in most plants it is accomplished by insects. In order to attract insects, the flowers have showy white or brightly colored petals. The base of the petals usually secretes a concentrated sugar solution called nectar and often there are aromatic substances also. Some insects like perfumes too!

RAYS may produce seeds. Rays surround the tightly packed disk flowers in the center of such composites as daisies, and each ray may produce a seed at its base. Composites vary in this. In some, each ray will produce a seed while the disk flowers in the center are all sterile. In other composites, the rays are all sterile and the disk flowers produce seeds. In still others, both rays and disk flowers produce seeds. See sketch of Composite Flower.

EXCELLENT LOCATION

The Rocky Mountains are a splendid region in which to look for flowers because the altitude varies from 5,000 feet to over 14,000 feet, and many plants grow only at certain altitudes. With plant life, altitude corresponds to latitude. This means that by driving from Denver to the summit of Mt. Evans, you find flowers and trees similar to those you would see on a trip through Wyoming, Montana and Canada to the Arctic Circle. Going up 200 feet in elevation corresponds roughly to driving north 70 miles—about 1 degree of latitude.

This explains why there is such a wide variety of flowers in the Rocky Mountain region of the United States.

Also many of them can be seen for long periods. Most flowers grow in more than one zone, so on the same day one kind of flower—say Springbeauty—may have stopped blooming at 6,500 feet but at 7,500, it might be in full bloom, and at 8,500 feet you may find it in bud.

HOW MANY KINDS OF FLOWERS IN THIS REGION?

There are probably around 3,000 species in the state of Colorado. A majority of these could be definitely identified only by botanists, usually with lens, because aside from technical differences, they look so similar to other species. And they have no common names.

Many flowers are infrequent to very rare. This book includes over 475 of the most common or easily recognized flowers in Colorado.

The Rocky Mountains lie in part of 7 states: Montana, Idaho, Wyoming, Colorado, Utah, New Mexico and Arizona. Some plants grow only in certain sections of these mountains. But many of the flowers listed here (either these or very similar species) are found not only throughout the U.S. Rockies but also in the Canadian Rockies to Alaska, as well as in the Black Hills of South Dakota and the Cascade and Sierra Nevada Mtns. of the three Pacific states. Some grow in northern countries around the world.

ENDANGERED

Rather than pick wildflowers (most of which wither very quickly anyway) how about taking pictures, which never wither? Or keeping a notebook record of the flowers you have found? Thousands of people visit the mountains every week in summer. If each of them picks just one flower—especially if the roots come up with the flower—what will be left in a few years for you to enjoy?

There is a wonderful flower garden in these mountains but it urgently needs protection.

REFERENCES

Booth, W.E. and J. C. Wright
1959. Flora of Montana, Montana State College, Bozeman, Montana.

Craighead, John J., Frank C. Craighead, Jr., and Ray J. Davis.
1963. A Field Guide to Rocky Mountain Wildflowers, Peterson Field Guide Series. Houghton Mifflin Co., Boston, Mass.

Davis, Ray J.
1952. Flora of Idaho. Wm. C. Brown Co. Dubuque, Iowa.

Harrington, H.D.
1964. Manual of the Plants of Colorado. Sage Books, Denver, The Swallow Press, Inc., Chicago, Ill.

Kelly, George W.
1970. A Guide to the Woody Plants of Colorado. Pruett Publishing Co., Boulder, Colorado.

Long, John Chenault
1965. Native Orchids of Colorado. Denver Museum of Natural History, Pictorial No. 16.

Manning, Reg
1970. What Kinda Cactus Izzat? 20th Printing. Reganson Cartoon Books, Phoenix, Arizona.

McDougall, W.B.
1964. Grand Canyon Wild Flowers. Museum of Northern Arizona, Flagstaff, Arizona.

More, Robert E.
1949. Colorado Evergreens. Denver Museum of Natural History. Popular Series, No. 9.

Nelson, Ruth Ashton
1979. Handbook of Rocky Mountain Plants. Skyland Publishers, Estes Park, Colorado.

Patraw, Pauline Mead
1951. Flowers of the Southwest Mesas. Copyright by the Southwestern Monuments Association, Santa Fe, New Mexico.

Pesman, M. Walter
1967. 7th Ed. Meet The Natives. Denver Botanic Gardens, Inc., Denver, Colorado.

Roberts, Harold D. and Rhoda Roberts
1959. Some Common Colorado Wild Flowers. Denver Museum of Natural History, Pictorial No. 8.

Roberts, Rhoda and Ruth Ashton Nelson
1957. Mountain Wild Flowers of Colorado. Denver Museum of Natural History, Pictorial No. 13.

Shaw, Richard J.
 1969. Wildflowers of Yellowstone and Grand Teton National Parks. Wheelwright Lithographing Co., Salt Lake City, Utah.
Standley, P.C.
 1926. Plants of Glacier National Park. Government Printing Office, Washington, D.C.
Thornton, Bruce J. and H.D. Harrington
  Weeds of Colorado. Agricultural Experiment Station, Colo. State University, Ft. Collins, Colo. (Bulletin 514-S)
Weber, William A.
 1976. Rocky Mountain Flora. Colorado Associated University Press, Boulder, Colorado.

INDEX

INDEX

INDEX

INDEX

INDEX

INDEX

INDEX

INDEX

RECORD SHEET

Date	Place	Flower	Comments

RECORD SHEET

Date	Place	Flower	Comments

Please send me a copy of
The BEAUDOIN EASY METHOD OF IDENTIFYING WILDFLOWERS

_____

Name   (Please Print)

_____

Address   Apt. #

_____

City   State   Zip

I am enclosing $_____

Enclose $8.95 per copy. Check or Money Order
Send orders to: **Evergreen Publishing Company**
1665 Nome Street
Aurora, Colorado 80010

Please send me a copy of
The BEAUDOIN EASY METHOD OF IDENTIFYING WILDFLOWERS

_____

Name   (Please Print)

_____

Address   Apt. #

_____

City   State   Zip

I am enclosing $_____